START HERE

START MORE THAN YOU CAN FINISH

A Creative Permission Slip to Unleash Your Best Ideas

WRITTEN AND ILLUSTRATED BY

BECKY BLADES

CHRONICLE PRISM

Library of Congress Cataloging-in-Publication Data
Names: Blades, Becky, author.
Title: Start more than you can finish / by Becky Blades.
Description: San Francisco, California : Chronicle Prism, 2022.
Identifiers: LCCN 2022006269 (print) | LCCN 2022006270 (ebook) | ISBN 9781797216133 (hardcover) | ISBN 9781797216140 (ebook)
Subjects: LCSH: Goal (Psychology) | Achievement motivation. | Success.
Classification: LCC BF505.G6 B53 2022 (print) | LCC BF505.G6 (ebook) | DDC 158.1--dc23/eng/20220214
LC record available at https://lccn.loc.gov/2022006269
LC ebook record available at https://lccn.loc.gov/2022006270

Manufactured in China.

Design by Brooke Johnson and Becky Blades.
Illustrations by Becky Blades.
Author photograph by Jenny Wheat.
Typesetting by Maureen Forys.
Typeset in Gilroy and Tiempos Text.

10 9 8 7 6 5 4 3 2 1

Chronicle books and gifts are available at special quantity discounts to corporations, professional associations, literacy programs, and other organizations. For details and discount information, please contact our premiums department at corporatesales@chroniclebooks.com or at 1-800-759-0190.

CHRONICLE PRISM

Chronicle Prism is an imprint of Chronicle Books LLC, 680 Second Street, San Francisco, California 94107

www.chronicleprism.com

Dedicated to teachers,
who rarely get to see
their finished work.

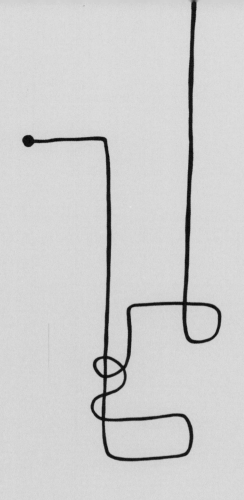

a Line is a Dot that went for a WALK.

PAUL KLEE, ARTIST

a line is a Dot
that wasn't Afraid to get STARTED.

— Becky Blades, stARTist

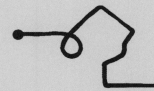

CONTENTS

INTRODUCTION

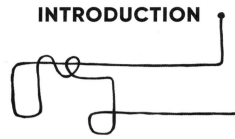

The people who raised you thought they were doing the right thing.

When they told you not to start what you couldn't finish, they thought they were helping.

When they said, "If it's worth starting, it's worth finishing," or "It's not what you start, it's what you finish," or even "Don't bite off more than you can chew," they thought they were planting lifelong guiding wisdom that would make your dreams come true.

I'm guessing the people who lodged these tropes in your head were not worrying so much about your creative destiny as they were about you leaving a mess lying around. They were afraid of crayons between the sofa cushions and half-constructed cakes in the kitchen.

Maybe they were afraid that if you didn't finish your homework, then you'd never finish your tax returns, and then one unfinished thing would lead to another and you'd be sleeping on their sofa in your thirties. They were afraid you'd build bad habits that would ruin *their* dreams for *your* life. In other words, *their* fantasy finishes.

I'm just spitballing here, because no one said these things to me.

My dad was kind of MIA, and my mom had six kids and a job, so she forgot to worry about crayons in the sofa. And she forgot to tell me to finish everything. In fact, my mom said things like, "You're never going to finish that macramé dog poncho; maybe you can make it into a hat."

And look! I arrived safely at adulthood without poking my eye out or marrying an axe murderer. In fact, I'm living a lusciously messy creative life.

The things we think without thinking have an oversized power over us.

And these particular auto-repeat tracks in our heads—clichés that say finishing is everything and that a start without a finish is moral failure—they don't do the job they intended.

Likely, these tropes don't make us *finish more*, they just make us *start less*.

In a world that demands our creativity, what we say to each other about starting and finishing can be warped and often harmful. Whether it's telling our dad not to start another lawn sculpture before he's sold his first three or telling kids not to get out the Legos before dinner, placing guardrails around initiative is the opposite of encouragement. It douses creative courage and stunts our growth. And it matters.

We need to start more.

We ALL need to start more.

We ALL need to imagine things and push the ignition switch to begin them.

We need to start things that will take ten minutes and things that will take five years, and things we will never, ever finish.

Because acting on our ideas is the best of who we are.

If you have ever hesitated to start something because you weren't sure you could finish it, this book is for you.

If you have ever had an inspiration die on the vine because you didn't pick it and begin it fast enough, this book is for you.

I stARTed THIS foR YoU

If you have ever nixed a fun idea fearing it wouldn't be perfect or profitable, this book is for you.

If you, in your head, invented the carrot spiral kitchen tool thing but never made millions of dollars when it became AS SEEN ON TV because somebody else got to it first, this book is for you.

If you have ever been asked, "Whatever happened with that thing you started?" only to hang your head in shame because no, you did NOT ever finish that thing, this book is for you. Not because it will ensure you finish that thing—although that is definitely a possibility—but because shame about finishing gets in the way of starting. And I think I can help.

I wrote this book to ask you to leave MORE YOU in the world.

Isn't that what we all want? To make our time here matter? To leave scraps of ourselves behind so that years from now when the aliens land they just might find the poetry club manifesto we wrote in seventh grade and say to one another, "Wow, these organisms were feisty."

We leave ourselves in the world in so many ways—in how we raise our kids, how we treat people, how we make a living.

But this only scratches the surface. I have come to believe that the truest and the most vivid way we leave ourselves in the world is seen in how we act on our ideas . . . in the things we make, deliberately.

The value in acting on our ideas is not measured in grand, planned finishes. The value is in each and every start.

1. THE SUM of OUR stARTS

Adding up unfinished business and the magic of a third-grade seating chart

I was chatting with a group of business leaders at a cocktail party, focused on balancing my glass of chardonnay on my appetizer plate, when someone brought up a name I recognized.

It was the name of a serial entrepreneur, a person I respect. He's an energetic mover and shaker, a community supporter with an innovative mindset, a civic asset. So imagine my confusion when this small, elite group proceeded to skewer him, in that "Well, since-you-bring-it-up . . ." sort of way.

"He's great, really smart, but . . . he's always launching some new thing—always full of new ideas. Did he ever get that building renovation off the ground? I mean, just asking . . . what has he actually *finished*, well . . . besides his first company?" Others piled on.

Keep in mind, this was Kansas City, birthplace of "Kansas City nice," so the talk was polite and full of feigned affections. But make no mistake, it was judgy.

I don't remember many cocktail conversations, but I can't shake this cruel and critical memory. Probably because these people could easily have been talking about me.

I had sold my first company a couple of years earlier, and I was not setting the world on fire. I was chairing the board of the agency I sold my business to, but I was, let's be honest, 100 percent unnecessary. Mostly, I was having fun playing creatively—experimenting in my art studio, writing articles and poetry, and diving into civic projects.

I had sold the business so I could do those sorts of things, but I was starting to think it wasn't enough. That conversation, among businesspeople I had once tried so hard to impress, crystalized doubts I'd already been having. *Am I spending my time the right way? Am I going to finish the projects I've started this year? Is anything I'm doing important? Am I a quitter? Or a one-trick pony?*

Later that week, with my fiftieth birthday approaching, I decided to take an inventory of all my unfinished projects. I told myself it was a motivational exercise—that I was administering tough self-love in order to make myself finish more of the things I started. Time was running out, after all. Tick tock, old lady. I felt the need to horrify myself—and worse, to shame myself—about all the creations I had left unfinished at this, life's halfway point.

This creative audit would be the reality check I needed to make the most of the second half of my life. If I felt the real pain of my failures, I would be scared straight to success, and to more finish lines, baby!

So on my birthday, I started counting.

I started with my writing failures. I dug into old computer files and trudged down the memory lane of my touch-and-go literary career. I found scraps of work that never made it out of the draft folder: poems with missing stanzas, articles that never found a publisher, and the really bad novel that, trust me, we are all better off without.

I did a separate review of my art life. I ransacked shelves to find paintings I had abandoned, printmaking experiments from workshops, and half-finished sketches of my kids. I found carefully constructed sections of sculptures and chunks of wood taped to power tool pamphlets. I found project folder after project folder . . . thirty years' worth.

With every found project, I tried to remember why I had started and what was going on that kept me from finishing. For days on end, I visited my former self to ask her what the heck she was thinking.

"So I see you started an article about collecting Fiestaware. Where, exactly, were you going to pitch that? Did you get tired of writing, or did you just get a phone call?"

"This painting of Tess . . . she looks to be about ten years old. If I recall, you started this to show her how to draw eyes. Nice job."

"So, about this drawer of jewelry-making supplies with the two half-finished bracelets . . . did you just forget it was here?"

I asked, and then I listened.

Well, sometimes I argued. When I found the sketch for a painting of my now-dead dog, fourteen unsent thank-you notes, and a promising travel article, I shook a shaming finger. *How could you abandon an idea after putting so much into it? This could have been something. You should have stayed with it.*

When I found a journal with 150 pages of a handwritten memoir I began in my twenties, I trudged through the insufferable, self-indulgent angst. It should have been titled *Poor Me*. I was so smart and hardworking, yet so unappreciated. How could the world be so cruel? After berating the twenty-three-year-old writer and patting her on the head, I recalled that I abandoned that memoir, not because it was vapid and juvenile (oh, it most definitely was), but because I had decided—thank goodness—that I could never put something so salacious out into the world while my sainted mother was still alive. This sent me apologetically back into the journal, looking for valuable forgotten tidbits of my youth. It was there that I found the story of a third-grade girl and a bulletin board that I had completely forgotten for nearly thirty years—and that opened the portal of creative memories that inspired this book. Sit tight, I'll tell you more on page 26.

During one day of computer rummaging, I found the business plan for a consulting firm, which never got off the ground, and I became angry at all the work I had put into it . . . until I read, contained in it, the precise words that became the value proposition of the public relations firm I was to begin a few years later, the company that was the delight of my career.

After weeks made up of moments like these, days of foraging, and hundreds of arguments with myself about old work, something unexpected happened.

Much like the end of a weekend-long lovers' fight, I declared an exhausted truce. I had reconnected with my younger creative self. I had said ugly things I could not take back, but lo and behold, the love was still there, stronger than ever. And we had worked out some important ground rules going forward. I would not berate my young self for her scattered interests, for her short attention span, or for not setting up a decent filing system, and she would stop telling me I was too late—for anything.

I still had more work to review, and I had no intention of stopping. But the process had changed.

You see, what I expected to make me feel crappy and terrified was making me feel just the opposite. I felt inspired and jubilant. I didn't want it to end. Revisiting my life's unfinished business was downright exhilarating.

What started as a cruel kickoff to a midlife crisis turned into an epiphany. Bringing ideas to life, even those that didn't work out, had been the most elevating, illuminating act of my life. I didn't see any of my starts as failures. I saw them as the building blocks of my creative process. I saw them as my mind awake.

In each beginning, I saw growth. I saw a writer growing more direct, more colorful, and a lot less wordy; I saw a businessperson learning to assess ideas and risk. I saw an artist grow from timid to fearless.

My midlife audit was cause for celebration: that in a life with all the stuff life is made of—laundry and bills and work and broken plumbing—I had found time to breathe life into some ideas. **I had found the time to try, and to wonder, and to play . . . and to act on my curiosity about whether things could look as good in the world as they did in my head.**

With the benefit of hindsight, I saw success. I saw clearly how an idea that didn't get fully executed when I was twenty-two had inspired something better when I was thirty-two, and how a small project pivoted to something bigger. I saw creation after unfinished creation become a vital link to a later breakthrough.

It turns out all my unlaunched businesses, unhung art projects, never-assembled clubs, unthrown parties, unpublished essays, and assorted unfinished beginnings each served a completely complete purpose.

I felt a lot of emotions as I walked through my creative past, but regret was not one of them.

Finished starts are delightful. But not everything we start may reach the finish line we plan for it, and that's okay. Because each start serves as . . .

- **A LAUNCHING PAD** for other projects, other ideas
- **A CONFIDENCE BUILDER**, giving our brains proof that what we imagine, we can ignite
- **A REALITY CHECK**, vital proof of what happens when we move from concept to real world
- **A GPS PATH**, directing the brain to the next insight
- **A HEALTHY DIVERSION** for the brain's frontal lobe
- **EXERCISE** for our starting muscles: flexibility, vision, risk tolerance, and more
- **THE FIRST STAGE** of a wildly successful creation that we could not have conceived without this step

After weeks of counting, I declared a finish line and stopped counting my unfinished projects at . . . 2,865.

That's if you count social media posts, my kids' baby books, and my mom's eightieth birthday bash (to be fair, she pulled the plug on that one; I was 100 percent ready to go).

So yep, that's the number: 2,865 times I started a thing and did not, technically, finish it. That's a lot of loose ends.

Here is where I should mention that I've finished some things, too. Among those thousands of starts are completed, celebrated accomplishments.

I've **built** companies—a communications firm, where I made my living for much of my career, plus some smaller side ventures: a publishing company, a real estate business, a fashion accessories line, a tiny travel company, and a not-very-techy tech company. All of them made SOME money except one. I'll tell you the not-so-sad story in chapter 6.

I've **made art**—from driftwood sculpture for my garden to mixed-media wall-mounted art sold in galleries. I've **written** things. After twenty years of essentially ghostwriting for other people in my public relations work, I've **published** articles, books, and poetry, and artful clarifications for several people I caught being wrong on Facebook.

I've **created** textiles, like garments, accessories, and the world's longest piece of handmade fringe. (It's more interesting than it sounds.) I've **produced** events, fundraisers, presentations, and training programs; I've even cowritten and produced a song, just to say I did in this book.

Like all of us, I've completed parties, trips, meals, emails, photo albums, and a gazillion thank-you notes that were full-on creative masterpieces.

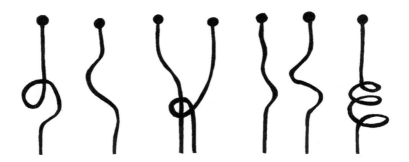

Without a doubt, my unfinished work played a part in all of my finishes—a sneaky, snarky, elegant, diligent, courageous, and excruciatingly essential role. I might never have known this if I hadn't gone scouring through my past.

Making peace with my starts and finishes set me on a course that clarified my life's direction and escalated my creativity. Within a few years of my creative audit, I had *finished* more than 1,200 new things: products, artworks, writing projects, a song, two comedy shows, and this book.

We Are the Sum of Our Starts

We probably shouldn't count and tally where creativity is concerned (she says after a long story about counting and tallying creative things). We shouldn't assign value comparisons to the invaluable. But we do it. Not so much with numbers as with abstract private equations we construct to make our lives make sense . . . to steer ourselves to happiness . . . to endure our regrets. I do this tallying less and less, but when I do, it's with a new, empowering belief:

We are not the sum of our failures and missed opportunities, or our unfinished work. Nor are we made only of our big wins, the handful of things that turned out just like we wanted.

We are the sum of the imaginings we ignite and our ideas acted upon. We are the curiosities we chase and the potential that they illuminate in us.

We are the sum of our starts.

OUR STARTS
ARE SELF-PORTRAITS.

Pushpins and Construction Paper

I've had a front-row seat in every classroom since the first grade. It's not because I wanted to be the teacher's pet or make good grades. I sat in front so I could hear the teacher, because I had lost all hearing in my right ear in a bout with the mumps.

The first day of third grade, it became clear that this seating arrangement would be a problem. I was a fast worker, and I liked to talk—especially to Janet with the go-go boots, two seats away. Also, I struggled with what I now know was attention deficit disorder (ADD), though we didn't talk of such things back in the late sixties.

Imagine little Becky in the front row, finished with her math assignment, fidgeting and shout-whispering to Janet, loud enough to distract all the kids still trying to do math. This was not front-row behavior.

It's a good thing my teacher was a genius. Mrs. Beehive (not her real name) shut down the madness in the second week of the school year with one brilliant third-grade teacher move: She put me in charge of the bulletin board.

In case you're not impressed, let me explain that the third-grade bulletin board of George B. Longan Elementary School was not a little 5-by-8-foot (1.5-by-2.4-meter) placard of corkboard. No, no, no, friends. This was the bulletin board dreams are made of. It ran the entire length of the classroom front to back, then it turned the corner to continue for half the width of the back of the room. I'm guessing it was 5 feet (1.5 meters) high and no less than 10 linear yards (9 meters) of creative blank space. Channel your inner eight-year-old and tell me that doesn't take your breath away. It was SO large, and *I* was in charge.

I had so many places to start, and so few boundaries. I had no deadlines and no finish lines. I wasn't graded or compared to anyone else. I just did my thing.

Rest assured, the teacher got everything she wanted out of the arrangement. Mrs. Beehive had some must-posts—calendars, science charts, pictures of dead presidents, the usual. But this boring stuff needed themes, colored paper cutouts, and marker-traced busy towns, and all of this, my friends, ALL OF THIS was up to me.

If I had to pinpoint when I first knew I was creative, that making things makes me tick, it was those days working on the third-grade bulletin board.

I channeled my interests and stayed out of trouble. Instead of talking to Janet with the go-go boots, I cut out go-go boots and arranged them in George Washington's footsteps to cross the blue-construction-paper Delaware River. Instead of sitting in my seat biting my fingernails to nubs, which I was known to do, I traced my hand and cut out a gazillion hands to build a border around the bulletin board.

Talk about facing a blank page every day! I had so much bulletin board real estate to cover that **every crazy idea I came up with had a place to go**. I started a new idea or theme practically every day, changing sections with lesson plans, seasons of the year, and parent open houses.

I learned to work in short bursts, make quick decisions, and do work-arounds when supplies ran out. When holidays hit or seasons changed, work got intense, so I built processes, templates, and one-girl assembly lines. I knew exactly how many autumn leaves I could cut in a stack with a pair of dull school scissors. I learned to clean up quickly, so I could get back in my seat as soon as the class moved to a new lesson.

I know what you're wondering. Weren't other kids jealous? Didn't they want to play too? This was one of the most magical parts. Either I was so absorbed, or Mrs. Beehive was so skillful, it never came up. Occasionally, when another kid got fidgety in class, Mrs. Beehive asked me to give them a project. It cramped my style a bit, but it helped develop some much-needed social skills. For the other kid, I mean.

As queen of the bulletin board, I felt important and empowered. I had a ready pipeline of art supplies, permission, and autonomy. I had an ever-present muse and a healthy distraction. I forgot about not having my own go-go boots and about the tall-girl taunting I endured from cool George M. and mean Steve T., and I almost forgot the deep shame of our family television being broken during the first weeks of *Gilligan's Island*. There's no time for ruminating on crushing child-hood disappointment when you've just had a breakthrough with yellow pipe cleaners and Elmer's glue.

More started on that bulletin board than met the eye. Decades later, I can see that a style of art emerged that is still evident in my work today. I still use collage and layered cutout materials; I still love whimsical houses and silly trees. And I still find cutting leaves out of paper to be a meditative labor.

Most of all, from that great big, colorful, messy cork pincushion, a view of life emerged: Every day, after the math is done, it's good to start something creative.

The world is a great big bulletin board and you can't possibly finish it.

That's okay. Because, as I hope you'll come to agree, finishing is not always the point.

I hope you unleash your "stARTistic" powers by filling up your world as I filled up that bulletin board—with abandon, passion, and luscious imperfection.

I hope this book does for you what Mrs. Beehive and that bulletin board (and also maybe my midlife crisis) did for me:

- **BUILD** your starting muscles
- **CHANGE** your ideas about finishing
- **INSPIRE** ideas that only you can start
- **LEAVE** more YOU colorfully pushpinned all over our world

START HERE, if you want to.

I want this book to meet you where you are—to help you grow, grow, grow and go, go, go! Or, to let you relax and read while I convince you that you're doing great; your self-portrait is gorgeous and you don't need to be a tech mogul or Instagram influencer by Thursday.

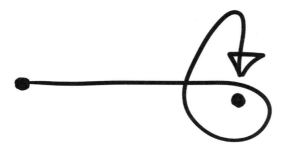

So I've designed some exercises, as exercise. It's functional exercise—to move the muscles you'll need to move your ideas.

For you go-getters ready for **more than training**, I put the exercises in order to help you move your idea from *what if?* to *work-in-progress* fast. By chapter 8, or Tuesday, whichever comes first.

Pick your approach: You can read the whole book, including the exercises, then come back to work through them later. Or you can work through exercises as you go, by choosing an idea and making it your stARTistic case study. (Picture me standing, nodding, and slow clapping in respect.)

I bring no tests, no grades, no shame. Just a permission slip to roam the halls of your imagination and start a thing that inspires you.

MAKE YOUR STARTING JOURNAL

(5 TO 20 MINUTES)

1. **Get a notebook.** No need to get fancy. A spiral notebook from the school supply aisle can be better than the arty journals you got for your birthday. Or maybe you'd prefer a three-ring binder, to add and subtract pages.

2. **Get creative.** Design a journal you'll want to use. Put inviting art or words on the cover. Spray it with lavender.

3. **Get organized.** Inside, you'll want to be able to find things. Loosely divide the journal as you use it, or set it up in advance. Those stick-on file tabs from the office supply store can be a game changer.

Dedicate separate pages or sections to

- Ideas

- Exercises

- Things you start

- Things you finish

- Starts you pause or leave unfinished, with reasons why

- Starts that turn into something else (these are SO great to document)

- Big starts (leave twenty or more pages for each big idea as you launch it, or get a notebook for each project)

4. **Get real.** You're writing for your eyes only, so don't hold back. Journals change lives and ideas. They're private conversations with ourselves that help us light a path for our thoughts and our best work. Go all in!

Journaling can net stunning health benefits, especially when we get reflective and expressive. Research shows that regular journaling improves mood, confidence, and memory and even boosts immune cells, lung health, and liver function, just for starters.

Use your Starting Journal for the upcoming exercises in this book, but don't stop there. Make it whatever kind of magical touchstone and accountability coach you want it to be.

2. stARTistry

The reachable, teachable art of beginning

Starting can be hard. It's true. The fear of starting something new can keep people in jobs they hate, relationships that don't work, and homes with no closet space.

And it's why there are graveyards full of songs never composed, buildings never built, books never written, and businesses never launched. Honestly, it's why we can't have nice things—like world peace and self-ironing blouses.

Most of us, it seems, have decided that starting something new takes big energy and resolve. **We think it takes more than a normal amount of courage.**

Because starting something new in the middle of an already busy life seems risky. We can be paralyzed by the thought of a start that doesn't work. We worry we'll be wasting our resources, or revealing our true unfinished selves to people who think we have it all together.

But not all of us.

For some people, starting is not hard at all. For these people, starting is joyful, energizing, and downright addictive. They do it every day. They make it look annoyingly easy.

I call these people stARTists.

stART·ist /stˈärdəst/
noun
a person who takes creative initiative to start, restart, reinvent, or renew

stAR·Tis·tic /stärˈtistik/
adjective
relating to or characteristic of beginning creatively

stART·ist·ry /ˈstärdəstrē/
noun
skill or ability to begin quickly and creatively

The stARTist embodies the fusion of two dynamic qualities: creativity and initiative. These might seem to come as a pair, but we've all seen their solo acts: Some people eagerly take initiative but only by the book, within the lines. And some creative people overflow with ideas that never get actualized.

For stARTists, it's a single movement.

stARTists create. And they take initiative to do it.

stARTists take initiative. And they do it creatively.

To me, taking creative initiative means keeping art in the process—an open, expressive, beauty-seeking, iterative, out-of-the-box quality that makes the work uniquely ours. (That's why it's so tempting to capitalize the "ART" in stARTist. I do it often, just to remind us to keep ART in our starts.)

We needed new vocabulary anyway. When we say someone is a "starter," we may be implying they don't finish. When we call someone a "stARTist," we suggest that beginning is an art form. I like the second one!

As creative initiators, stARTists are proactive and good at . . .

- Taking risks to try out ideas
- Working independently
- Exploring alternatives
- Solving problems
- Adapting to situations
- Thinking imaginatively, laterally, with few constraints
- Making connections and combinations
- Articulating ideas

Some of these abilities are natural personality traits. But they're by no means fixed or set, behavioral psychologists assure us. This isn't hardwiring.

When they embrace and lean into these copiloting strengths, stARTists are all vessels of dazzling potential.

You'll know a self-actualized stARTist when you see one:

- **A STARTIST SEEMS TO BEGIN NEW CREATIONS AT THE DROP OF A HAT.** They get ideas, assess their viability in split seconds, and start bringing them to life.

- **A STARTIST HAS WELL-TONED STARTING MUSCLES AND HEALTHY ATTITUDES ABOUT FINISHING.** They act on their ideas, because they know their ideas deserve it. And if they don't have an idea, they use the ideas of others to solve problems, fill voids, and create beauty.

- **A STARTIST MAKES OBSTACLES PART OF THE PLAN.** They approach beginnings with a creative process and open-mindedness that turn fear into productive excitement.

- **A STARTIST IGNITES IDEAS WITH CURIOUS CONFIDENCE.** They know that once they begin, anything can happen.

are stARTists MADE or BORN?

(LET's NOT geT Ahead of OURseLVes.)

stARTists in the Wild

So who are these people I call stARTists? Do you know any of them? What do they eat for breakfast?

For starters, they're who you would expect: most every artist, entrepreneur, writer, inventor, and architect. They're all those people who make their livings walking up to a blank page or a bare canvas or a business plan. They're the people working in the creative jobs.

Every field that requires beginning new projects requires stARTistic skills: stARTists are teachers, chefs, engineers, event planners, marketers, community leaders, landscapers, fashion designers, decorators, and web developers.

Strong stARTistic muscles are always a plus in these jobs, and often, they're essential. In these fields, the most stARTistic practitioners are the most successful: They think big, try new things, and stay current and curious.

And what about those careers that **seem** to be creativity-optional? Those nuts-and-bolts jobs that require us to hold the line, dot the *i*'s, cross the *t*'s, get the right answer, and keep to plan? Can we find stARTists in these jobs? What about accountants, administrators, lawyers, electricians, and farmers? What about salespeople, custodians, and cashiers?

Absolutely, stARTists are there, too. Why wouldn't they be? Creativity and initiative are key to productivity and problem-solving. Creativity shows up in critical activities that we take for granted— from conversations to coordinating schedules. And initiative is the ticket to advancement in most any field.

True, some jobs don't require facing a blank page or acting on our own ideas, but jobs are a small part of who we are.

If you're an accountant who writes poetry or a lawyer who makes jewelry or a factory worker who makes music, you've likely seen the surprise when people learn of your "other" life. This just shows how much we typecast one another with job identities and education.

There's no degree or curriculum for creative initiative. We learn it in the wild.

You see, it's the absence of guardrails that fosters creative initiative. When we have to figure things out on our own, our missteps and miscalculations build adaptability and problem-solving skills, the cornerstones of creativity. And initiative is built not by being guided to start and finish, but rather by the opposite— by having to assert control and power to get things done, usually because nobody else is there to do it. This doesn't mean that being neglected as kids makes us better stARTists, but it does mean that a free-range childhood of making our own fun is better stARTistic training than, say, college prep in pre-K and overscheduled summer vacations.

Are YOU a stARTist?

1. Do you start more than you finish?

2. Do you ever begin something new before you have finished a previous project?

3. Do you feel 100 percent of sound mind when you drop everything to build a hydro-powered critter air gun for the squirrels digging up your yard, even though you're on deadline for a work project?

4. Have you ever started a business or a new product, service, or division within a business?

5. Have you ever started a club, class, political movement, or sports team?

6. Are you a painter, a sculptor, an architect, a chef, a writer, a filmmaker, or an inventor?

7. Have you ever thrown a party?

8. Have you ever taken an art class?

9. Do you have a creative hobby?

10. Did you ever buy a book about starting more than you can finish?

This was a trick quiz. Of course you're a stARTist.

But if you answered "yes" to two or more of these questions, you're more than that. You're a curious, self-aware stARTist who is already on page 39.

Oh, you may not feel like a stARTist yet. Or worse, you may feel like being a stARTist is a curse instead of a superpower. You're in the right place.

WHEN SOMEONE
ASKS
if you're a
stARTist,
ALWAYS
say
"YES."

Kindergarteners and Scientists Agree

Ask a room full of kindergarteners in a room full of art supplies "Who's an artist?" and every kid will have one hand in the air and the other reaching for a paintbrush. There may even be a stampede.

If only we grown-ups had such eager certainty when invited to declare ourselves stARTists. Sadly, somewhere between kindergarten and adulthood, many forget that when we say "yes" to creating, we say "yes" to a primal source of bliss.

So I'm here to remind you. As a bona fide nerd on the science of the brain and creativity, I can confidently assure you that the experts agree with the kindergarteners: **Starting makes us happy. But that's just the beginning.**

Over the past thirty years, clinical psychologists, neuroscientists, neuropsychologists, behavioral therapists, and others have studied the benefits of creativity. Evidence keeps building: What goes on in the brain when we're beginning something new is downright life-giving.

New experiences, new information, new efforts . . . they fire up those power places in our brains and release all the feel-good chemicals: endorphins, dopamine, and serotonin. The benefits are more than short term. Some behavioral scientists recommend everyday creativity as a path to contentment and "flourishing." Creating makes us healthier, happier, more hopeful, and even smarter.

Starting new things treats the brain to safe little surprises. It stretches our senses. It awakens transmitters that have been asleep from relaxing into routines for too long. Neuroscience has the receipts—on video.

What is NOT going on between our ears during the starting process is even more fascinating. You see, when creativity is in full crank, clock watching is not going on, self-monitoring is not going on, critical judgment takes a break, and other negative emotions we're prone to are scared away by our amazingness.

Yes, science proves that we can drive our own well-being by living creatively. And it doesn't give us extra points for finishing famous or making money from our art. The benefits come no matter the size of our projects or whether we finish on time.

Here's where to start taking notes.

When we add what we know about the science of creativity and happiness to what stARTists show us about starting and finishing, we get a big aha: Happiness doesn't come from finishing everything we start. Rather, stARTistic bliss comes when we **1) celebrate all our starts, 2) embrace all forms of finishes, and 3) trust the creative process to make our best work.**

If you want to learn about the neuroscience of creativity and happiness, check out my favorite resources in the Recommended Reading section on page 251.

CELEBRATE YOUR STARTS

(5 TO 20 MINUTES)

1. **Title a page in your journal "Starts of a Lifetime."** Begin listing your starts—things you remember beginning, whether you finished them or not. For now, just list five to ten. Leave some room between items, in case you want to come back with notes or doodles later.

2. **Write quickly about each item with a positive, playful tone.** Why did you start? Why are you glad you did? What did you learn? What would you have missed if you had never started? Did your start lead to something better? Did it make you happier or a better person, if even for a little while? Say how your initiative and creativity enriched you or defined you.

3. **Explore the unfinished things.** Do you recall why you didn't finish? Don't go looking for regrets, but if they pop up, write them down. Is *not finishing* your only regret? Maybe you got everything you needed just by starting. Would you finish it if you could?

4. **Make room for more.** Title the next five pages: "Starts of a Lifetime." As you recall more starts from your past, or make more in the future, come back and list them. Take the time to draw whatever inspiration your starts have to offer.

FOR ADVANCED CELEBRATORS . . .

5. **Make art of your starts.** Package, assemble, or display your started ideas like the treasures they are.

   For visual work, save a section of the piece, or take a photo to one day become part of a slideshow or a photo collage. For non-visual starts that live in a computer document—like a business, article, or comedy routine—get creative! Print a passage on fabulous paper, roll it into a scroll, and tie it with a leather string. Make a meme, a collage, or a smash book. Make a recording, a gif, or a mashup.

   Delight in your starts and let them take up space. The time may come when they inspire a finish.

3. StARTeR MeNU

Barbecue dreams, lean startups, and hungry art students reveal the delicious possibilities

Counting my starts and finishes refreshed my memory about my creative past. It satisfied my curiosity about the contents of some dusty flat boxes, about my past work processes, and about what became of my youthful longings.

This clarity soon sparked a new curiosity; it sent me on an odd quest to learn about other people's unfinished business.

It was easy to learn that da Vinci and Picasso left legions of incomplete projects among their finished masterpieces, that Einstein was still working on the unification of physics on his deathbed, and that *Little Women* author Louisa May Alcott left one of her first novels unfinished at age seventeen and never went back to it. Didn't we all?

But I was curious about people still alive today. What are they leaving on life's cutting room floor, and how do they feel about it?

Are they feeling shame? When they think of their unfinished creations, do they feel like failures? Are they listing finished projects on their resumes and hiding their unfinished work? Does getting stopped by life's roadblocks make people less stARTistic? I asked more than two hundred people of diverse backgrounds, interests, and ages how they felt about starting and finishing. What I found was interesting, but not surprising.

1. **MOST OF US DON'T FINISH EVERYTHING WE START.** And we often feel bad about it.

2. **PEOPLE WHO START MORE DON'T FEEL AS BAD** about not finishing.

3. **ALMOST EVERYONE HAS SOMETHING THEY WANT TO START,** something they've conceived and contemplated and still wistfully wonder about, which they have not yet begun.

What Aren't You Starting?

If a stranger you would never see again asked you to tell them about something you intended to create, what would you say?

Sometimes, I like to be that stranger.

My "stranger" conversations started by chance several years ago with a young man I met in a restaurant. We were both traveling solo and were seated at the tiny, close tables along the wall they give you in big cities when you're a party of one. From that short distance away, the man saw me doodling in my journal. "Are you an artist?" he asked. "Yes," I said, in a friendly tone, but with no eye contact. I had "peopled" enough that day.

"I wish I was creative," he replied. "I'm a banker. Ha ha ha."

I smiled. Mostly because the server was arriving with my fish tacos, giving me an easy end to the conversation. Is a quiet lunch too much to ask for?

A few minutes later, the man's brisket arrived, and he said, out loud as if we were dining together, "I know, New York is not the place to get barbecue, but I had a craving for beef."

Well, I'm not a monster, and I *am* from Kansas City, the barbecue capital of the world, so I chatted. Turns out, Tom was from Oklahoma and was under the impression that *he* lived in the barbecue capital of the world. So we had plenty to talk about.

With appropriate deference to me, a woman fifteen years his senior, Tom let me know that he knew a thing or two about barbecue. He had built his own smoker and grills, and was known to throw big "feeds" in college and now in his small town. His specialties were pork short ribs and burnt ends slathered in his own secret sauce, which had won rave reviews in a Tulsa cook-off.

"I thought you weren't creative," I said.

"Oh, I'm not," he said. "I just love cooking and making things for my friends. I can't draw a stick figure or carry a tune."

I could tell Tom had said these words before. They were a well-rehearsed package. So in response, Tom received my well-rehearsed package about creativity—that it's not just art and theater, that we're all creative beings, and that acting on our ideas is the essence of a creative life.

I reminded him that he had built grills and smokers.

"Oh, that's not creative. I got plans and kits from the internet."

"What about the parties you throw? And the food you make? Isn't that creating?" I asked.

He didn't see it that way. "Lots of people do those things. I'm not the first person to throw a big barbecue."

"Okay then, what about your sauce?"

A huge grin spread across his face. "Well, you got me there. My sauce is a work of art."

Then, genuinely curious, I asked him if there was something he wanted to do that he hadn't started yet.

"Yes, actually," Tom said. "I've been wanting to start a barbecue cook-off—a contest to get the big barbecue judges to come to our town."

He explained that there were lots of contests, but none in his county. "And mine would be different," he said. "I have some ideas."

Then he talked excitedly for ten minutes about backyard teams, judging systems, and the merits of barrel smokers. I sat nodding while Tom convinced himself that his cook-off idea deserved a shot and that he should probably get on it before the spying pitmaster one county over got there first.

I don't know whether he started his cook-off event, but I will tell you this. As excited as Tom was about that event, it belongs at the top of his "started" list.

You should get three other things from this story:

1. A lot of stARTists don't think they're creative.

2. A lot of people have things they want to make that they are putting off.

3. Kansas City is the barbecue capital of the world, no matter what the guy from Oklahoma tells you.

The world is full of people like Tom, with ideas stuck on "unstarted." Here are the top ten unstarted creations, according to my personal invasions of people's privacy, hundreds of interviews, and a thousand responses to SurveyMonkey.

1. A book

2. A house or other structure they build themselves

3. A work of art

4. A business

5. A home remodeling project

6. A video, film, or screenplay

7. An invention

8. A group, a club, or a convening event

9. A course or curriculum to teach

10. A fashion creation (clothing, jewelry)

What about you?

What would you tell a stranger once they outed you as creative? What happiness-making, heart-healing, world-fixing, barbecue sauce–slathered thing have you been keeping in the "someday maybe" file?

Or are you just craving to create, to make something by you, of you, for you? **Are you a stARTist in search of a start?**

Sometimes we're hungry, but we don't know it until we look at a menu. So what sounds good?

You could start a big bold creation or a new variation. You could start . . .

an Instagram post · *a well for a village* · a ship in a bottle
· a pear orchard · **A LOVE LETTER** · a musical
· **an eco-friendly apartment building**
· a humanitarian relief effort · a llama ranch
· a study group · **a lemonade stand** · a compost cooperative
· a fun uncles cookout · a doodle art exchange · **a grant application**
· a fusion soup recipe · a balloon animal class · an auto body shop
· a comedy sketch · A TOUR OF YOUR TOWN
· A MUSICAL · a thesis · **a donkey rescue** · a greeting card line
· a yarn bomb · *a flag* · a humanitarian relief effort
· a jewelry line · a tree farm · **a button club** · a supper club
· a toy · a light show · A ROBOT RACE · **a gratitude chain**
· **a preschool** · a lake house · *a manners class*
· a vegetable garden · AN ARCHAEOLOGICAL DIG · a drone parade
· a fashion line · **a kayaking race** · a front porch movement
· *a neighborhood watch group* · A PRAYER CHAIN
· a curriculum · a conversation salon

- **a cure for shingles** • an empty-nest support group
- a Legos build-off • A ROSE GARDEN • a family
- a remodeled fireplace • a documentary • **a veggie burger recipe**
- a _____-of-the month club • an apartment recycling program
- **a food desert fix** • a lace hanky
- a better mousetrap • **A BOOK COVER DESIGN** • a syllogism
- **a vineyard** • a law • a time-saving process • a street mural
- a children's chorus • a sonnet • *a halfway house* • a hook rug • a blog
- a poem • A NEIGHBORHOOD GROUP • **a composting co-op**
- a painting • a sculpture • a journal
- A PARTY • a tea salon • **a safer bungee trampoline** • a vegan hotel chain
- **a new language** • **a historical tour of a cemetery**
- A CHAIN HUG • *a rolling pin collection* • a fast casserole franchise
- a philosophy • a family manifesto • **a think tank**
- a fitness club • AN ARCADE • a wildlife reserve • **a saddle club**
- a basement renovation • **a learning society** • an urban play place
- a pun throwdown competition • an umbrella repair shop
- **an antique car exhibition** • a diplomacy clinic
- a photography retreat • **A BIRD SANCTUARY** • a comic book
- **a woodworking shop** • an artist's retreat • A PORTRAIT
- a chain reaction • **A BREAKFAST CLUB** • a network • a focus group
- A MAKERS SALON • a short story
- **an animal therapy practice**
- a hubcap sculpture • *a welding class* • a pottery collective
- a horse arena • **A CHURCH** • a camp for middle schoolers
- a café • *a magazine* • an editorial board
- A HUNTING BLOG • a fragrance
- *a trail ride* • a log cabin • a culture blog

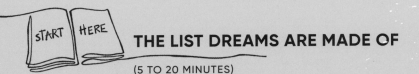

THE LIST DREAMS ARE MADE OF

(5 TO 20 MINUTES)

1. **Name a thing you want to start.** In your journal, write the idea that comes first to mind. What sounds interesting? Or fascinating in its audacity? If you bought this book with a specific idea in mind—a life goal that you want to get the ball rolling on—fabulous. Give it a name.

2. **Think harder, and write four more.** What notions have crossed your mind that didn't feel worth your time at another stage of life? What sounds easy? What sounds impossible? What ideas would you like to see made real in the world? What would you like to tell your best friend you made?

3. **Keep going.** What would you start if you had everything you needed? Choose some tiny ideas. Choose some tall orders. This list won't have a finish, so don't sweat it. Keep listing. Choose ideas from the list on pages 50–51, and add some from your own imagination. Pretend you have all the time in the world and that "done" is not what you think it is.

Creative Excuses

You know who have interesting things they want to start? Art students.

Young humans who decide to go to art school for college, with fire in their spirits and their whole lives ahead of them, seem like the most stARTistic people alive. That's why I love hanging out with them. They're kooky, they're on the cutting edge, and where else can you learn the best dumpster-diving spots for art supplies?

For a few years, I guest lectured to a class of aspiring illustrators at the Kansas City Art Institute. They were seniors, so by the time I met them, these kids had some things figured out. They knew what their education had given them. They had decided to be illustrators, not sculptors or weavers, and their parents were probably calling them weekly to ask what they were doing to find a job.

I talked to them about the job market and about getting their heads in the game to begin their careers. At the end, I gave a little survey. In a few progressive questions, I asked students if they had an idea they wanted to act on, and why they hadn't started it.

The results should not have surprised me. While the art students I surveyed are indeed natural stARTists, nearly all had specific and inspired things they wanted to create that they just didn't get to.

Why, exactly? They all gave essentially the same answer: They didn't have ENOUGH.

Of what, you ask? I smoothed off the edges of their wonderously rambling answers, made some inferences, and put the answers on a matrix. These stARTists—young people studying creativity as their life's work—said they did not have enough . . .

1. Time
2. Resources
3. Space
4. Confidence
5. Skill
6. Clarity
7. Permission

The students' ideas ranged from sweet and simple to grand and glorious: a mural on an overpass, a children's book about a lost blind dog, a graphic novel about a dysfunctional family. Each had clear, specific ideas. But, they said, they hadn't acted on them . . . because they didn't have *enough* to trust they could see them through.

I've also talked to dozens of writers and entrepreneurs, and lots of friends I've cornered at parties too close to the bar to mount an escape. Even the most confident, risk-taking stARTists give largely the same answers: **They don't begin things because they're not sure they have ENOUGH to finish the job.**

These are never short conversations, mind you. Creative people like to talk about their ideas. They like to talk about how the next groundbreaking art series is worked out in their head and how they will definitely do it if they win that two-month residency they applied for three years in a row. If they feel defensive, they'll talk about how if they lived in a bigger city or their great-aunt didn't need them to bring groceries, they might have more control of their schedules, or about how, you know, the dog ate their first draft.

Creative people get creative when they're pressed for excuses.

When I saw an irrefutable trend in their answers, I became intrigued.

I added a question to the class survey and even pulled some students aside individually to ask, "So, you don't have enough to finish your (insert idea). Do you have enough to just *get started*?"

I asked them to forget about finishing for the moment and to think about how they would begin.

"What does a first step look like? Would you begin by sketching and measuring? Would you begin by sourcing materials? By pulling a team together? Would you start with competitive research?"

"Forget for the moment about whether you have the last gallon of paint for the mural or the license to put it on the building, or a place to stash your paint clothes when you go to your barista job. Do you have enough to START?"

Again, their answers were similar: "I don't know. Maybe."

I've learned that "maybe" always turns into "yes" when we talk a while longer.

They have a lot in common—the banker who denies he's creative but loves to feed his friends barbecue and the people studying to make creating their life's work.

They're sitting on ideas that should absolutely, positively be part of their stories. They're keeping ideas inert that they could put in motion. All the while, they're spending their initiative and creativity on assignments from other people.

If you're one of these people, start flipping your script.

Instead of thinking about all you need to get your idea to a big finish, think about what you already have to begin it.

Creative Start-Ups

If we wait until we're sure we have all we need, we're probably waiting too long.

Entrepreneurial stARTists teach us this. They find ways to begin companies before their full vision is completely funded. Sure, money is always part of the fuel businesses need, but you can't get on *Shark Tank* without some proven success.

That's why businesses start as sidelines, weekend gigs, and garage projects. Creative entrepreneurs find the

time and the space to begin, even when they have no idea what the finish looks like or where the resources will come from.

When I started my first business, a public relations firm, my husband and I made a deal: I could go six months without bringing home a paycheck. We could squeeze by with credit cards for that long. I couldn't use any savings, because we didn't have any.

My company, Blades & Associates, had to get creative with start-up costs. So I traded out services for rent in the back offices of my last employer and subleased office equipment from them. I even shared ownership of my new company, selling a small percentage of stock to a few trusted mentors. I created a situation with very little risk. I didn't have enough to start the agency of my dreams with a fancy reception area and assistants for my assistants, but I had enough to start.

Our first revenue came from overflow work from my former employer, thanks to the deal we had struck. Our second client came quickly: the tiny town of Fort Scott, Kansas. The Chamber of Commerce wanted to draw tourism to the town and its claim to fame, a historic military fort. They had $1,500 a month to spend, the tiniest budget I'd ever worked with. It was the very definition of a starter client. They thought we were eager and adorable and that we'd work harder for them than a big agency. We were. And we did.

Our third client was a big law firm, and the fourth was a small airplane manufacturer. We were on our way.

One client led to another and the company grew. As it turned out, I didn't have to go a single month that first year without a paycheck. Within a few years, I had bought out my investors and we were in our third office expansion with a roster of national clients. We employed twenty-five full-time staff and a dozen contractors. Still a small company, but it was more than I ever set out to build.

If you had told me when I started that I would have a monthly overhead in the six figures, **I might have been terrified. I might never have started.** The risk would have been unacceptable. I'm guessing it would violate all the Suze Orman/Dave Ramsey credit formulas. And my husband would have been a hard sell. Having our house as collateral on a business loan when the monthly expenses exceed the mortgage, well, that's not how he rolls. But that never happened.

Looking back, I can see that at thirty years old, I didn't have enough *confidence, money,* or *know-how* to plan a company as big as the one mine ultimately grew to. I did not yet have the *track record* to earn the size of clients we ultimately earned. I could not offer enough *opportunity* to attract the *powerhouse staff* who made it the award-winning company it ultimately became.

But I had enough to start. And within a few short years, our team had enough of all those things to innovate with bigger and bigger clients, and to attract talent partners to keep our agency growing.

Every business is unique, but there wasn't much that was innovative about our business model. It was a simple fee-for-service agency. But the way we began felt innovative and exciting. We loved finding ways to make do on the cheap: shopping used office furniture stores, training talent just out of school, improvising with guerrilla marketing and creative scheduling. **By starting with what was available, we started sooner, scaled leaner, and built a scrappier culture.**

Thousands of successful companies are launched by people with no cash reserves, no employees, no equipment, and no office space.

By contrast, thousands of companies go out of business that are richly funded, deeply staffed, with huge R&D budgets. Resources don't ensure success.

Research Shows:

Humans don't FINISH 100% of the Things We DON'T START.

Enough to Start

We can all lock into limited thinking about what it will take to bring ideas to life. We've been taught that the foolproof way to make a thing is to work backward: Begin with the end in mind. Make a plan and have everything you need from the get-go.

But art and businesses are not dressers from IKEA. We can't be sure which parts and pieces we'll need, or what we'll have when we've used them all.

We can only know what's required of the first step. And we can only know the first step when, if only briefly, we loosen our demands on the finish.

Do you have enough to start?

Let the question bend your mind a little. Forget for the moment whether you have the confidence or the time or the room in your basement to make a mess. Try saying "yes." When you get stARTistic

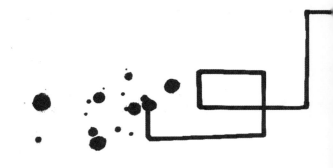

and discover how little money, time, help, and room you actually need, any place becomes a starting place.

Think about one of your own ideas—a thing you want to make or do. Do you have enough to START bringing it to life?

I'll bet you do.

To the writer who claims she doesn't have *time* **to write her book:** "Do you have fifteen minutes a day to journal about what's holding you back? To play with ideas or characters?"

To the social change agent who doesn't have enough contacts to build the coalition she needs: "Do you know one person to call who might know one more person to call?"

To the broke art students who aren't starting their murals: "Can you start sketching and colorizing your mural before you have the *wall* and the *client* and the *money* for the paint?"

Yes. Of course you can. And very likely, it's the same way you'd start if you had all the resources standing by.

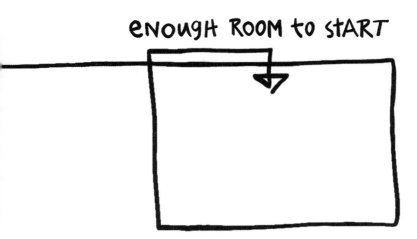

enough Room to stART

Are We Done Here?

By now, some readers will be stoked to get their new restaurant or tricked-out drone idea off the ground, and some will be squirming—worrying that I'm letting quitters off the hook and contributing to the de-gritting of a generation.

Please don't miss the obvious. A stunning, bigger-than-imaginable, completed creation is abso-flippin-lutely what I want for your ideas, and mine. No question. Finishing is the end game. Done = good. FINISHING IS ALWAYS ON THE MENU.

Let's also agree that . . .

- NOT FINISHING is a choice—an acceptable choice, and a choice we can only make after we've started.
- NOT FINISHING is NOT failure.
- The ACTUAL FINISH is rarely what we envision at the outset.
- FAILURE HAUNTS THE FINISH LINE; focus on a specific finish gives power to the specter of loss and disappointment, stealing creative courage. In fact, fear of completion comes largely from fear of failure.

"I'm just getting started!" is our jubilant rallying cry before we let failure into our thinking. It means "I don't know where this is going. I'll figure it out." It means there's room for innovation and crazy ideas. It says "Leave me alone, I'm trusting the creative process."

START HERE

FIND YOUR ENOUGH

(15 TO 30 MINUTES)

1. **Declare your start.** Open a computer file or journal page for one of the things you want to start/make/do that you haven't yet begun. The BIG THING, if you have one.

2. **Name the project.** Fast. Something fun.

3. **List everything you need.** What resources do you need to complete the project? Be as general or specific as you want to, but you only have ten minutes. No research allowed.

4. **Find three ways to start now.** What steps can you take with what you already have? (Examples: a sketch series, collaboration meetings, an outline, a list of partners)

5. **Keep it handy.** Put this page or file it in a place you can find it quickly. You'll be taking it for a walk.

I'll demonstrate:

1. I want to start a welders-who-drink-chardonnay success group.

2. I'll call it WeldedWiners.

3. I will need:

   - A partner (I am too busy to do this alone, and I only know two other welders who will cop to drinking white wine.)

   - Welders, and their actual contact information

   - A place to meet

   - A mission statement (This isn't critical, but it will be the most fun part, so let's do it.)

4. I can start today by:

   - Listing places to find welders

   - Calling the friend I made in the welding class I took in 2006 to ask if he wants to partner with me

5. I'm saving this document in my journal, snapping a photo of it, and starting a computer folder titled "WeldedWiners."

4. The PARTS of OUR stARTS

How we imagine, think, decide, and act to give an idea its pulse

Starting is a skill. And like any other skill, it can be learned, practiced, and mastered. When we do it right, we can go anywhere, start anything. If we fail to learn it, or we teach it to ourselves wrong, our whole creative life can be stunted.

Don't let me scare you off here. You see, I've geeked out on this topic, so you don't have to. Instead of spending hours populating my Pinterest boards, I've studied why some people spend hours populating Pinterest boards with driftwood art they want to make while others spend hours actually making driftwood art. I've figured out why starting is easy and energizing for some while terrifying and exhausting for others.*

It's more complicated than "Just do it!" but it's simpler than we think, because in one way or another, we're already doing it.

Starting something new has four distinct phases or stages or steps, or what I'll call simply "parts." I didn't make them up.

Check out the Recommended Reading on page 251, if you want to get knee-deep in the neuroscience and brain scans.

They're phases that psychology experts and behavioral scientists tell us that humans go through when we make change in our lives or create something new:

Part 1: Imagine

Part 3: Decide

Part 2: Think

Part 4: Act

Straightforward, right? You get an idea and imagine what it will look like, you think about it, decide what to do with it, and then take action. Simple-sounding parts. But each simple-sounding part is as complicated as the person and the project.

Let's talk about how most people do these parts, then we'll talk about how stARTists do them.

Part 1. Imagine

Imagining is where we expand our thinking from what exists in front of us to what might be. To what we can add. Or fix. What we can bend or move.

To bring our imaginings to the real world, we package them in forms we can talk about. A notion. A vision. A question. A "what if?" An idea.

Much has been written through the ages about how ideas come to us. Some creators consider themselves mere channels for ideas, like the novelist who sits down and writes characters and scenes and plot twists, effortlessly, streaming ideas as if through high-speed broadband.

Some of us think ideas are treasures for which we are ever on the hunt. We keep our eyes peeled for combinations and epiphanies that will be ours to possess if we get there first.

Some scholars think quite clinically about ideas, reasoning them, in most cases, to be the brain moving chemicals and transmitting energy to fill in a gap or subconsciously solve a problem.

Some people believe ideas are visions and fusions of facts we stumble upon as we try to satisfy our longings.

Still others believe ideas to be gifts of a divine conversation, spiritual in origin. They believe that in creating, we take direction from the universe, or a deity, an ultimate muse.

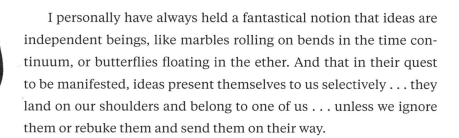

I personally have always held a fantastical notion that ideas are independent beings, like marbles rolling on bends in the time continuum, or butterflies floating in the ether. And that in their quest to be manifested, ideas present themselves to us selectively . . . they land on our shoulders and belong to one of us . . . unless we ignore them or rebuke them and send them on their way.

Part 2. Think

With an idea taking up space in our imagination, we are called to move it along. We either discard it as a figment or fantasy, or we walk it next door to that place in our brains that will figure out how to make it real.

If the idea is a small one, within our normal lives, we're all set up for this thought process. But if it's a big idea, like starting a business, a book, or a social movement, we have to think about both the idea AND what it will change in our lives.

Experts tell us that to make real commitments, humans must go through a stage of contemplation—a time to research and talk to others about our plans, a time to ponder, deliberate, examine, and mull over how this new thing might come into being. What might it require?

How many wine bottles will it take to build a glass house? Who should I interview to write that article about the pitfalls of dating a taxidermist? What size knitting needles would I use to yarn bomb the DMV? And what will my kids be doing while I'm doing the bombing?

The bigger the idea, the more we want to think on it. Once we're convinced an idea is viable, we might need still more time . . . time to dream and wonder, play out imaginary scenarios, and talk to all of Facebook and the nice lady sitting next to us on the airport shuttle, because she might know something, right?

Ultimately, the thought process takes us to personal questions:

- Do I have the time?
- Will I enjoy it?
- Will I persevere if I hit snags?

- Do I want to do this alone or get a collaborator?
- Will *having it done* be worth the *effort of doing it*?

And, if we're doing it right, thinking through our ideas takes us to the deepest question of all:

Who will I be if I do this, and who will I be if I don't?

Part 3. Decide

Ah, the decision. That moment we resolve there is no turning back. The majestic instant that we declare to ourselves that the research is done, the debate is over. This is going to happen.

The mental act of decision-making is a well-studied, even photographed, conversation between reason and emotion. It's a cognitive struggle between the parts of the brain that sort facts and those that weigh in with feelings. Neuroscientists know the paths and chemicals and brain parts to explain how one side wins over another to choose between one product or another, one college or another, one poker strategy or another.

Deciding to create a thing we've imagined is more complicated than choosing between two things. It's placing a bet on our future selves to make future choices . . . to balance facts and feelings with yet-to-be-known risks and rewards.

When we're deciding about something small that we know how to do, we can decide a quick "yes." But as ideas move into risky, long-term territory, things change.

Deciding to make a doodle sketch of my dog is easy. But deciding, for example, to host a yearlong podcast (which, rest assured, I have decided NEVER to do) would require betting on unknowns: Will I show up every week with ideas and energy? Will adrenaline be enough to call forth the reluctant extrovert within me? Will I have the confidence to recruit guests, select music, and fix tech problems when the techie quits without notice?

Our decisions to act on our ideas hinge on the things we pondered in the previous "thinking" part, plus our emotions, our histories, and maybe what was on the news that day.

Decisions are hard work. They're situational. Long-term commitments take longer; creative decisions are emotional. The phenomenon of decision fatigue—the theory that our decisions can get worse after making a lot of decisions—suggests that decisions can be exhausting and not much fun.

This is why, in my view, **we don't so much decide *against acting* on our ideas. We often just *decide not to decide.***

But making decisions is critical to a life well lived. We must make them, and when we decide to do a thing, we rule out the possibility of NOT doing it. We stand on the island and send the boat away. We change our story.

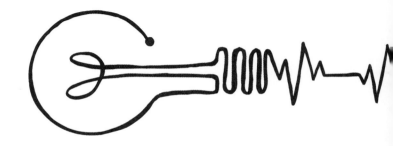

Part 4. Act

Imagining, thinking, deciding—they can all happen invisibly. Acting on our idea moves it out of our heads and into the world.

Action is energy we can see.

This is the moment when we light the fuse, flip the switch, open the valve.

Taking action sets up a shift in us, putting skin in the game and launching a kind of mental momentum. Action triggers what psychologists call the Zeigarnik effect—a tendency to remember unfinished activities better than completed ones. It installs our creation in our brain as a beacon that calls us back to it. Our project becomes an inspiration magnet, attracting information and attention, consciously and subconsciously. Inertia doesn't stand a chance.

If you've decided to start something, this is where you make it real.

Act.

Do something.

Give your idea a pulse.

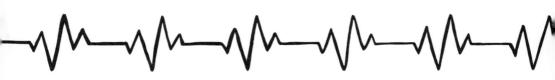

Moving Parts

Successful stARTists enjoy and master all of the parts of starting. Often, they can't explain how they do it. They don't always know where one part ends and the other begins, because they can move through the parts in nanoseconds. A stARTist can have an idea in the shower and decide to take action before she drops her wet towel on the bed.

By contrast, the struggling, stARTistically challenged—let's go ahead and call them nonstarters—might do each stage intently, laboriously, with excruciating focus and caution.

How do powerhouse stARTists speed through the four parts—to start bigger, better, and more often? And how do they imagine, think, decide, and act on their ideas, over and over again?

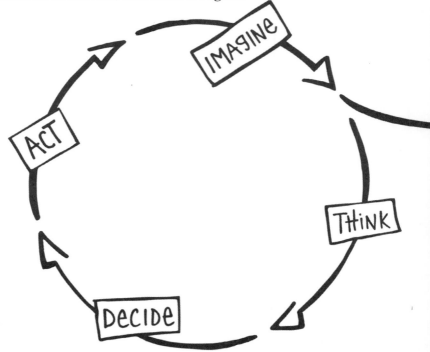

How do stARTists avoid the land mines of negativity that snag nonstarters? How do they bend life to their will to find joy instead of overwhelm? How do they juggle multiple projects and still find delight in starting that one more thing?

The answer is in the movement—purposeful, expectant, open-minded, integrated, curiosity-stoked movement through the four parts of the start.

The stages of creating are not linear; they're interconnected, fluid, and circular. The parts don't end or begin, but set up an ongoing process of iteration and regeneration.

Think about gears for a minute. A simple gear is a power switch with teeth on it. When you connect the teeth of one gear to the teeth of another, they move inseparably. As one turns, it turns the next in the opposite direction. Wait. What?! Yes, and each connected gear moves likewise.

When gears are different sizes, they change the power of the force moving them. So when you move a small gear that's connected to a larger one, you create an interrelated mechanical advantage.

This is what the starting process looks like.

Like gears of a novel machine, any part of the starting process launches a transfer of force that activates all parts.

When you take action on an idea, the gears of your inspiration and imagination engage.

The things you contemplated come into sharper focus. If they're obstacles, you see how easy it is to discard them or work around them. If they're opportunities, you see details of potential in neon.

As your idea becomes real motion and energy, it encounters information from the real world—details and possibilities that may take you back to your imagination, perhaps forcing another decision, more exploration, more energy.

As long as you keep it moving, this zany machine is producing power—it's producing your idea, feedback, and new layers of information, and it's powering the not-yet-formed ideas to come.

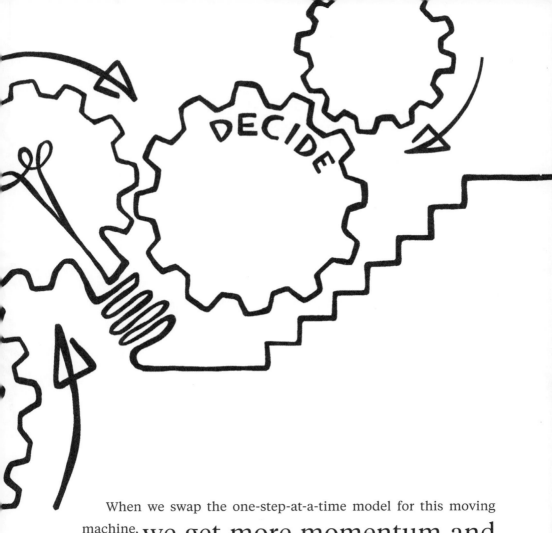

When we swap the one-step-at-a-time model for this moving machine, we get more momentum and power, less fear and regret.

The delight of this machine is not that we produce a hundred widget-shaped widgets per hour, but that we produce a lifetime of moving masterpieces.

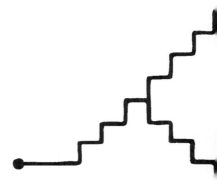

But we were told there would be steps.

I know, steps seem easier. Stacked in order, all the same size. It's crisp and tidy. You can view it this way if it's working for you. But the words we assign to our processes make a difference.

Here's how I see it: stARTists do all the steps, or parts, but not always in order. And they may skip steps, or do them so quickly they seem imperceptible.

A stARTist can make a decision to start a project, then go back and look for ideas and inspiration. Like the playwright who decides she'll write a play for an upcoming festival, but has no idea what she'll write about.

A stARTist may still be pondering a decision when he takes action to move the idea along. Like the gardener who is thinking about tearing out and replacing a flower bed and begins separating plants and sketching ideas before the decision is crystal clear.

A stARTist may be already started on a project when they return to the core idea and reimagine it. Like the entrepreneur who starts a sewing lab to make money and reignite the fashion industry in her community, then decides to turn it into a not-for-profit teaching at-risk women a job skill, and then pivots to making protective masks during the pandemic. (True story!)

And, of course, stARTists change their minds. With little or no shame, we step away from decisions, change our thinking, and start something else.

It's inspiring, because stARTists **start more**, and our starts **become more** because we imagine, think, decide, and act, all at once, in powerful ways.

5. StART LiKe a stARTist

Road trips, five-year-olds, new pilots, and comedy improvisers show us how to start more, better

My friend Laura Schmidt was riding shotgun in the family car on a long vacation road trip. Her husband was at the wheel, her three nearly grown kids were in the back seat, and she had kicked off her tennis shoes. She read a book, looking up now and then to take in the scenery and to keep from getting carsick.

This was in Kansas, so the scenery was mixed . . . billboards, then cornfields, more billboards, wheat fields, flint hills, an old barn, big trucks . . . highway signs and more billboards. Between cornfields, Laura's eyes landed on the toes of her socks, and an idea landed on her shoulder: Maybe socks would make good billboards. Billboards for the subconscious.

I should tell you that at the time, Laura was a very successful sales director for a national brand. Her success was owed, no doubt, to her enchantingly upbeat, encouraging, generous, supportive personality; she's one of the most genuine and loving people I know. She built her positivity habit through a lifetime of purposeful tools, including morning affirmations. So when Laura thought of socks as message boards, she naturally thought of positive affirmations.

IMAGINE
Like a
stARTut

Laura was a longtime student of affirmations. She used them in her parenting and in her work. In fact, the book she was reading on that road trip happened to be about the science of affirmations. She recalls that she had just read a passage explaining how the mind is most open to the power of words at two particular times of day, the times when we bridge from wakefulness to sleep: the first thing in the morning and the last thing at night—precisely the times when we're putting on and taking off our socks!

An idea visited Laura, fully formed in mere minutes, and she said out loud to her husband, "I think I'm going to put positive affirmations on socks."

She said the words "I think," but make no mistake, it was decided. Laura was making socks.

Laura had been deeply pondering her career for a couple of years. She had held her sales position for eighteen years, and she was ready for a challenge. So when the idea flew up to her, Laura grabbed it with both hands.

She thought about how to get her idea off the ground, how it would fit into her life, and how much risk to take. But she didn't think for long. Within days, she had made the decision to start a company, to begin making and selling socks.

Laura kept her day job, and she started small. She didn't indulge in market research or prototypes. They were not in the budget. She used the family credit card to order her first batches of socks: with "I am awesome" and "I am confident" knitted into the toes. Her daughter, then an ambitious high school volleyball player, wore them to a big match and gave the first thumbs-up review.

"I really felt it," her daughter Elaine says. "I wasn't thinking about it, but I had a great match, and when I took off my shoes and saw the words 'I am confident' on my socks, I thought, 'Wow, yes I AM!'"

That encouragement inspired Laura to imagine more. While she continued working full-time in her sales job, she leapt into full-on creative mode, pondering which words people most needed to believe about themselves and how they would best fit on a sock. She explored manufacturing, labeling, and packaging options. She named her company notes to self® socks and began selling socks from the trunk of her car.

The company grew. Soon she began calling on gift shops and selling online. She imagined sales displays and marketing campaigns. And slowly but surely, they worked. As Laura struggled to keep all the plates spinning, she imagined how satisfying it would be to focus full-time on her new company. She imagined how she might create jobs in her own community and a culture that would make people's lives better. Within the year, Laura took the plunge and put full-time focus on her new company. She operated from home for two years, then created Socks Central, the affirmation-stoked headquarters, warehouse, and fulfillment center.

Within a couple of years, her socks were being sold in Hallmark gift stores and other gift retailers, and notes to self® socks had appeared on the *Today Show*.

Today, notes to self® socks sells American-made socks, pillowcases, and apparel lines, with more than a hundred different affirmations, through hundreds of stores nationwide and a direct-to-consumer website.

Maybe Laura's idea to put affirmations on socks was floating in the universe with a homing device directed to a Midwestern woman who loves socks and needed a career change, or maybe the idea was the last piece of a puzzle Laura's subconscious had been working on for years. Either way, it was a big idea.

And because she treated it stARTistically, Laura made it a life-changing idea.

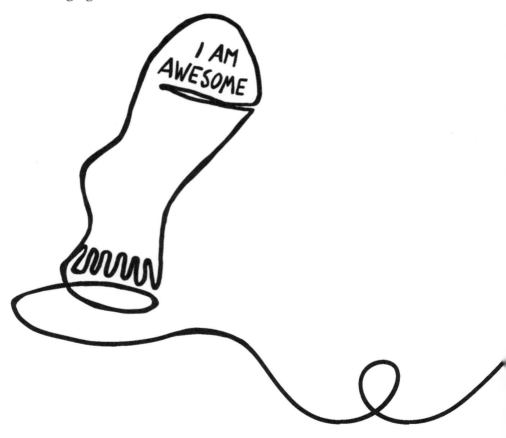

How do successful stARTists treat imagining differently? How do they get inspired, catch ideas, and transform them from wisps of thought to concrete expressions? How do they sift and sort the fantastical from the makeable better than nonstarters?

One big difference I've noticed: stARTists, like Laura, take their imaginings seriously. They're respectful. They're kind.

Have you noticed how very mean we can be to our ideas? Most of them we neglect, and oh so cruelly. And the favorites that win our attention, well, we expect way too much of them.

Would we treat human children like that? We don't expect our kids to ride a bike the first time they try, or learn to drive in a day, or become self-sufficient on graduation day. Sure, sometimes it happens. But mostly to other people's kids.

This was an epiphany I had when I transitioned from business writing to chase a creative writing career. I had spent my twenties and thirties working in marketing and public relations agencies. All my work had been assigned by clients, and when I had the freedom to write about ideas of my own, it was too much freedom. I got stuck. I came up with ideas for articles and essays, but then used all my creative strength to poke holes in them. In two years, I started only a few articles and didn't finish or sell any of them.

But gradually, after talking with other writers, and counting my unfinished work, I saw it. I was an idea bully. I came up with ideas only to pick them apart and steal their lunch money. Without giving them a shot, I decided they would never amount to anything. Instead of working to make the idea viable, I'd go looking for better ideas, and end entire work sessions with nothing to show. It was a pattern I had to break.

One morning I found an abandoned article idea in my unfinished file, titled simply "Bird's Nest." It was just a few sentences about a robin who built her nest on the transom over our front door. Twice before, I had run across the idea and been nasty mean to it. "What's so special about a bird's nest? Bird poop and clichés, that's all you are. I should delete you. You're a waste of iCloud space."

But that day, I decided to be nice—to my ideas and to my creative self.

I had just sold an article to Oprah.com and was working on ideas for a next piece. I wasn't in the mood to be nice, but I was on deadline, so I was kind of fake nice (that works too). As I scrolled through my folder titled "ARTICLE IDEAS" and saw the file name pop up, I literally spoke words out loud to my computer: "What are you whispering to me, little bird? Speak up."

I opened the file and sat with the idea for a moment. My mind wandered . . . first to the notion of an empty nest—my own empty-nest life with my daughters gone—and then to remembering how that robin's nest gave me comfort. Then, thoughts drifted to an article pitch I had written months before and never sent, titled "How to Convince Yourself It's Going to Be Okay."

I said a meek "thank you" to the idea and sent a pitch to the editor. That week, I wrote a little article titled "Whispers from the Universe That It's Going to Be Okay." In it was the nest idea:

FOR SEVEN YEARS NOW, A FAMILY OF ROBINS HAS CHOSEN THE EAVE OVER OUR FRONT DOOR TO BUILD ITS SUMMER NEST. When my two daughters were little, we used to spy on the birds through the transom window, watching the mother's spring nest-building through the weeks when she laid and guarded her eggs. We waited for the turquoise eggs to crack open, for naked, begging babies to fill the nest. Mostly, the robins delighted me, but as the novelty wore off, the nest became less of an enchantment and more of an annoyance. Smears of mud and grass stuck to the window, eggshells blew out and littered the porch, and then, of course, there was the poop. This past fall as my daughters left—one for college, one for her first big job in New York City—the symbolism of the nest struck me anew. One morning when I walked down the stairs and saw the empty nest through the window, I drew a deep breath, and tears came to my eyes. I sat on the stairs in front of the window and had my first good empty-nest self-pity cry. I had seen a mother create a home and push her babies out of it year after year, and it had never occurred to me that we had anything in common. In that moment, I felt one with every mother in the universe.

The nest idea was one little paragraph, not a full article as I originally imagined. But it jump-started a whole article. I was nice to the idea and it was nice back. The moral of the story is "It pays to be nice." In this case, $500. Thanks, Oprah.

We don't know when our ideas will be ready to fly. Sometimes our ready-to-start ideas are sleepy attempts we made years ago. Sometimes they're pieces of ideas left on the cutting room floor while we fine-tune other projects.

Today, I consciously treat ideas as if they are divinely directed to me, like they are newborn infants on my doorstep. I don't have to raise them, but I find them a safe place. I certainly don't tell them they're worthless.

Our ideas don't have to be darlings. They don't have to be well groomed, brimming with energy and immediate potential. Honestly, a messy, sleepy, just-awakened idea is adorable, and much more approachable.

We get better results when we talk to ideas in that voice we use with a bed-headed toddler, not with an insufferable teenager. "Good morning, sunshine. What would you like to do today? Do you want some juice?"

Before you know it, that sleepy idea is making its own bed and asking for the car keys.

Imagine your ideas want to get you where you're going, magically.

That's how stARTists do it. They kick off their shoes and look at the scenery. They let images and sounds wash over them, while letting their kids fend for themselves in the back seat. They read about things they believe in. They bring together what they know and what they're looking for.

They hold on to their notions and their first glimmers, keeping them where they can find them, to be inspired later.

A stARTist imagines . . .

→ *Always and everywhere*

→ *Possibilities before problems*

→ *Combinations, evolutions*

→ *Ideas becoming concrete, visual realities*

→ *As if the world will hand us everything we need to begin*

→ *Ideas that can heal, repair, and make things whole*

→ *Entire creations, even though our ideas may be full of holes*

START IMAGINING

(15 TO 60 MINUTES)

1. **Get your Starting Journal and your idea.** Continue with an idea from the earlier exercises, or select a brand-new one. Refer to the list on pages 50–51 if you need to borrow one.

2. **Start imagining and writing.** Some formats that help are:

   a) Write in the first person as if you've already decided to start the idea, such as "I will build a community garden, and here's why . . ."

   b) Write a letter to the idea, such as "Dear community garden, here's why I think you deserve a shot . . ."

   c) Write in the voice of your idea, such as "I'm a community garden. If you bring me to life, I can . . ."

3. **Take a walk.** Yes, go outside and walk in whatever way you're able. While you're moving, imagine that everything you know is wrong—your teachers were mistaken, your parents were asleep at the wheel, your friends are con artists, and nothing you believe is certain. What is it about your idea that opens up if all the rules change? Follow that bread crumb. Where does your idea go? Does it have more potential? Does it solve a different problem or take a different form? Can you start in a different place? Dictate your insights on your phone or write them down when you get home.

4. **Imagine what your idea will be when it's fully formed.** Be specific. Draw pictures if you want. What will it feel like to have brought it to life? How does your idea work on a small scale? How does it change if you expand it? What will change in your life or the world when the idea is complete or well underway?

5. **Ask questions and create scenarios to explore more.** Imagine a person responding positively to your creation. What would impress or surprise them? What would make their response even more meaningful? What could your idea be if someone with unlimited confidence and resources took charge of it? What if you were that person?

THINK

Like a

STARTist

Think Like a stARTist

The thinking part is not the innocent get-to-know-you meetup you may think it is. **It's the biggest variable in bringing our ideas to life.**

This is the stage where we look at the thing we imagined and contemplate what it will take and whether we're up for it. If your idea is going to get a bucket of cold water thrown on it, by YOU, this is the place.

Depending on what kind of stARTistic condition we're in, this can be the gear that moves all the others, or it can stop the whole machine dead on a dime. It can last nanoseconds, or it can last years. (Spoiler: We're shooting for the nanoseconds.)

Thinking done long is thinking done wrong. And thinking done wrong is dangerous. In some circles, it's called overthinking, and it's never a compliment. Wandering around in your own brain shopping an idea to yourself when all you have taught yourself to say back is "I'm not really creative" or "Sounds cool, but can you come back after I get my student loans paid off?" This kind of thinking has no place in the starting zone.

So hear me when I say: Until you're sure you're doing it right, don't think so much.

In-shape stARTists think fast and loose. They think with their gut. They think with optimism and a curiosity that makes them want to stop asking questions and start answering them on their terms.

I've come to believe that the people with the very best stARTistic thinking skills are people with a certain immaturity who have been proven to pull off whatever they set their minds to, even though they have no resources, no real authority, and limited patience. You know who I'm talking about: kindergarteners, again.

So, quick story. My husband, Cary, and I took our daughters to preschool music classes and after-kindergarten dance lessons. We were THOSE parents. We bought them little boom boxes and microphones and built a riser in the basement so they could be "on stage." We spent their early childhoods riveted and ready with standing ovations, no matter how rough the performances. We created stage-confident creatures who were missing nothing but an audience.

So it should have come as no surprise the summer when our girls were ages five and three that basement lip-synchs were no longer enough. Our tiny darlings wanted to be in a real show. Not just any real show, it *had* to be the musical *Annie*—their generation's version of *Frozen*, the musical they knew well enough to lip-synch seventy-two times a day.

No community theaters were holding casting calls, so we did the only thing we could. We started a theater. In the backyard. If I recall, the thought process took fifteen minutes.

As the venue owner, producer, and audience satisfaction supervisor, I thought I would be all-powerful in this start-up. I was mistaken.

Our five-year-old, Taylor Kay, did all the thinking and called all the shots. She was the producer and self-appointed casting director, and no one was surprised when the title role of Annie was awarded to Taylor by Taylor without the formality of an audition. She cast her three-year-old sister, Tess, in the role of Molly, whose sole job was to clutch a stuffed dog and look adorably adoptable.

Taylor was smart enough to cast every known neighbor child, ensuring the largest possible audience of parents and grandparents. Then, when I wasn't looking, Taylor cast me as Miss Hannigan, the cruel orphanage director who spent her stage time in a bathrobe and curlers, screaming at kids. (So, yes, I did this in front of my neighbors.)

In Taylor's mind, she had people for the roles, a costume box, and a karaoke machine. And she had a mom. All systems go.

Imagine, if you will, two rehearsals and wardrobe consultations led by a bossy five-year-old . . . a low-quality karaoke machine teaching lines to a dozen little girls dressed as circa-1930 orphans, shout-singing "It's a Hard-Knock Life," and scrambling through scene changes, wardrobe malfunctions, and technical difficulties. Imagine.

The Phillips Backyard Theater opened and closed its first production to a standing ovation and rave reviews. By that, I mean, no one asked for their fifty cents back.

I credit the success of this show to masterful stARTistic thinking, and by that I mean, *less* thinking.

Once Taylor had the idea, she did not ponder. When she imagined she could inhabit the role of Annie, she did NOT think of things that would get in her way or wonder whether she was up to the task.

She didn't fret about cleaning the yard or the transportation challenges of her four-year-old cast members. She didn't conjure hypothetical, imaginary horribles, like "What if twelve five-year-olds yelling off-key into microphones bothers the neighbors on a quiet Saturday afternoon?"

To this day, when I ask Taylor what she was thinking when she decided to put on that show, she recalls: "I just thought about how great it would feel to be Annie."

Not one brain cell went to work to help Taylor talk herself OUT of her idea. She relied on underlying beliefs that I'm guessing went something like this:

- Just because you've *never done it* and *never seen it done* does *not* mean you can't do it.
- If you need other people to pull something off, just make it fun and don't hold too many rehearsals.
- Trust what you know—in this case, "Mom won't let us flop if we give her a lead role."

Thinking like a stARTist means the thinking is mostly done when the idea shows up.

Take Laura's socks. The idea was a thousand little pieces of Laura coming together in spontaneous combustion: Everything she knew about affirmations, her passion for helping others, her confidence as a salesperson, her freakish love of quality socks (socks were her go-to gift for years), her parenting wisdom, and her longing for a career challenge all showed up to beckon and certify the idea.

All those parts of Laura needed only a passenger seat power chat, and she was ready to get ready.

She said to her husband, "I think I'm going to put positive affirmations on the toes of socks." She didn't ask his permission. She knew she was on to something and she wanted to do it.

A stARTist thinks . . .

- *Fast*
- *In motion*
- *With affirmations swirling in our brains*
- *Everything is possible*
- *"How can I?" and "Why not?"*
- *"I wonder what will happen if . . ."*
- *"What's next?" "What's next?" "What's next?"*

START THINKING

(5 TO 20 MINUTES)

1. **Write about the idea you're most excited about**—the one you imagined in "Start Imagining." Write in a Q & A format. For this first pass, don't do research. Answer with your gut, your best hunches.

   What are the first steps to make this real?

   What resources do I need to get started, roughly (time, materials, space, human help)?

   Who are people that will root for me and help me?

   How will starting this move me forward (career, skills, relationships)?

   Here's what's in my way of moving forward (obstacles), so how can I get it/them out of the way?

   What am I waiting for? What's the best time to start this?

Answer with honesty and compassion with the spirit of your inner five-year-old.

If you still have unresolved questions or obstacles, tell your brain to work on them while you're sleeping and doing mind-numbing life tasks. Make an appointment to come back to your journal tomorrow, or after several hours.

2. In a second journaling session, answer this question: *Why did this idea come to me and entice me?*

Use a full journaling session to explore why you and your idea found one another.

Example answer: "The idea of building a community garden entices me because I've enjoyed having a tomato plant on my back step, and I would love sharing the joy of growing and eating fresh vegetables with my neighbors. I'm good at figuring out what plants need, and I want to use this ability to help others. I imagine it would be meaningful work. And I'm curious. Every time I take caring initiative in my neighborhood, others step forward in surprising ways."

3. **Return to previous questions.** Write any new answers that have occurred to you, especially new possibilities, benefits, or true obstacles.

4. **Finally, if necessary, begin research** to fill in details you left unanswered about resources. If you're considering a big project that requires bids or complex sourcing of materials, decide what a first step would be if you *had* the needed resources.

For example, what if this was a project you were leading for a company and they had approved the budget? What would your first tasks be? Here's why: Getting the resources may be a step in the creative process that comes *after* you decide and take your first action. Doing it now may send you down rabbit holes that dampen your passion for the idea.

You need all your passion for the next part—the decision.

Decide like a STARTist

Decide Like a stARTist

So here you are. You're at the intersection of inertia and potential, and you've put away your phone.

You have an idea, and you've thought it through. You're curious and longing to breathe life into your creation.

Excellent. Now take this next step as fast as you can.

Declare it to yourself: The idea is worthy, and you will begin it.

There. It is DECIDED.

That's how stARTists do it. At least, that's how they *seem* to do it. It appears that stARTists decide quickly. They enjoy and examine an idea, then overlay it with information about what the first step might be. When it feels right, they press the "start" button.

Of course, there's more to it. It's a long, invisible process made of reason, emotion, and always . . . a backstory.

Deciding Moments

I was working at an ad agency hired by the general aviation industry to recruit future pilots. Airline travel was climbing, but the rate of pilots in training was dropping, threatening a severe pilot shortage.

Our agency started by researching the obvious question: If flying is so cool and pays well, why aren't more students signing up?

The answer, it seemed, was economics. People who very much wanted to take to the skies had decided it was out of reach. But research showed they were mistaken about the costs. Most people thought getting a private pilot's license would *cost* twice the money it actually did. And most thought training would take two to three years, when in fact a person could earn a license in about six months of weekends.

Our campaign had a two-prong strategy: 1) Get more people flying by getting the facts straight, thus satisfying their rational minds. 2) Close the deal with emotions, offering a discounted first flight—an exhilarating introductory lesson with the student in the pilot's seat. (Don't worry, instructors have dual controls.)

We declared June National Learn-to-Fly Month and hired as spokesperson Christopher Reeve, a real-life pilot the world knew as big-screen Superman. From the seat of his own Piper Cheyenne turbo-prop, the beloved icon (emotion) spread the down-to-earth (rational) message that learning to fly was fun, affordable, and worth the work.

My main job was getting stories into the media. One day, months into the campaign, I was at a tiny airport interviewing a flight instructor for a story. I asked him a question that must have sounded naive, and he shot me a look of befuddled alarm.

"What? Haven't you been up?" he asked incredulously.

He looked at his watch. "We can hop in the plane now. I don't have a student for an hour."

Gulp. I hemmed and hawed and mumbled something about a stomachache. He got the message.

Walking me to my car after the interview, he casually said, "If you're going to be doing this kind of work, you really ought to get your ticket."

"Ticket" is aviation slang for "private pilot's certificate," and I was starting to see how apt a term that was. In the industry, it seemed to be access to "the club," to credibility and advancement. As a young woman, I was beginning to see it as the ticket to be taken seriously.

Honestly, early on in the job I had the idea myself, of getting my pilot's license to make points with my bosses. But I dismissed it fast. Time and money were no small obstacles, but my real block was fear—of heights, of math, of getting lost over Kansas flint hills, and, of course, of failing.

With every passing day, however, I was getting curious. How might a pilot's license help my career? I imagined new benefits of learning to fly and new costs to saying no. My fear was subsiding, taking me from "Who am I to think I can do this?" to "Who am I if I *don't*?"

Economics says the "true cost" of anything is the forgone alternative—that is, what one *would have otherwise gained* with the same time, money, and energy. We used this principle to persuade students to follow their career dreams, and now it was seeping into my decision-making.

Later that week, I talked with my boss. He agreed to pay part of my lesson costs and give me time off for ground school. The economics changed. The cost of *not* learning to fly became bigger than the cost of lessons. It became a no-brainer. I decided to get my pilot's license.

You've heard people say, "If I had known what it would take, I would never have started." Usually, they're not saying they regret having done the thing. They're saying they're glad they didn't know all the facts, because they would have decided differently.

Well, that's what happened with my flying lessons. I believed my own press releases, which said flying lessons would be a six-month commitment. A girl can give anything six months, right?

Turns out, it took me TWO YEARS! My travel calendar caused scheduling hitches; I forgot material, missed ground school, restarted lessons three times, and changed instructors twice.

It was the right decision. But I'm glad I didn't know it would take two years, because I would not have trusted my future self to pull it off.

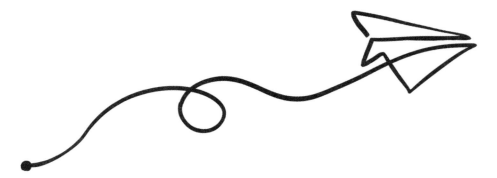

Remember, that's who we consult when we make big decisions—our future selves. We ask them whether they can deliver on our promises. We ask what they'll feel like on Saturday morning if they stay up late painting Friday night, and whether they'll be healthy enough in ten years to run a white water rafting company if we start today.

Which brings us to what we came for—help deciding whether to start acting on an idea.

Let's put this all together. We're clear that all good decisions come from complex chats and face-offs between **reason** and **emotion**. So when we decide whether to act on an idea . . .

We do the **emotional part** by predicting *how we will feel in the future* about our creation, whether we'll stay at it, love it, resent it, etc. Warning: Our future selves are clueless. They think they're going to feel close to the same way we feel right now. If we ask them again in an hour after *we've* had a sandwich, they may have a different answer.

We do the **rational, reasoned part** by weighing the *true cost* of our creation, which we can do only if we know *precisely*. . .

- What our creation will be, and how the process will affect us
- How we would use that same time and energy otherwise

Warning: We can't possibly know these things.

So, here we are. An idea has landed on us, making us eager and curious. *Not starting* it will have costs: regret, unknown possibilities, and a lifetime of wondering what might have been. We can't trust our future selves, we can't know what our creation will really cost, and we can't believe our own press releases.

There's only one answer, but it's a good one: We decide to trust the idea and the creative process.

It's not as scary as it sounds. First, remember, we're deciding just to **start**.

Also, there's a huge difference between deciding to act on our own idea and deciding to, say, take flying lessons. With our own creation, we're *really* in the pilot's seat. We tailor our creation to our reality in real time, letting the creative process hand off the work to our future self in tiny increments. Some stARTists trust this process so much, they actually let their ideas make the decisions.

"When an idea comes to me strongly or responds to something I've been thinking about," says an entrepreneur and chef, "the idea IS the decision. Oh, I'll do some 'gut checks,' but I don't go through a big process deciding whether to do it, just how to do it best."

A visual artist says, "Sometimes I'll get an idea that seems divinely inspired, or the answer to a longtime longing. I don't need to ponder it. The decision to do it has been made sometime in the past. My job is to work out the details."

A vineyard owner says, "My mind knows better than to give me an idea not worth acting upon. Once an idea hits my brain, I'm off to the races!"

If something feels right, stARTists lean into "yes." We can't start EVERY IDEA. But we can decide faster, with less anxiety, to start more.

A stARTist decides . . .

→ *To trust our ideas and the creative process*

→ *To bet on our future selves*

→ *With curiosity*

→ *How to spend our moments by knowing how we want to spend our years*

→ *Confident in our control over the true cost of acting on our ideas*

→ *Better and faster with practice*

→ *To lean toward yes*

START DECIDING

(15 TO 25 MINUTES)

1. **Decide how you'll decide.** First, write a deciding rule. Define your emotional criteria for saying yes to an idea, and actions you'll take, even if you're busy.

Example: "If an idea feels intriguing/exciting/fulfilling and (fill in goals/criteria), I will . . .

- Say yes to starting it (add timetable)

- Journal about it (add timetable)

- Add it to my ideas list

Go back to this page often to update your rules and add more. Our deciding rules change as we do.

2. **Use your new rule with your best idea.** Go back to the earlier idea you've been thinking about and apply the new criteria. Does it pass the test? Is it exciting? Is saying "yes" still scary? Does it make you want to revise your rule? Write about your feelings; this is a moment of insight.

3. **If you say "yes" to your idea, declare your decision.** On a new page, describe the commitment you're making, complete with happy shouts and emojis. Find those colored pencils.

I will start _____ (what/when/how) _____!
I'm excited because _____.

ACT
Like a
StARTist.

Act Like a stARTist

It might surprise us to watch the processes of some of the artists we glorify as they take the first action steps on their creations. It probably doesn't look elegant and organized. Likely, they move with a question mark in one hand and an eraser in the other. But they move.

Because stARTists know that starting feels like action.

Once a stARTist decides to bring an idea to life, we act swiftly, boldly, and imperfectly. We leap into action, often before we're ready and before we're certain what to do first. So yes, it might be messy and awkward.

What is a good first action for a new idea? Here's one test: Does your first step feel like you're moving and making something? Or does it feel like filling out forms? Or waiting for permission, or for paint to dry?

The first action is the invitation for the next one, so make it bold. Painters, make a grand brushstroke. Writers, write a dramatic exchange of dialogue. Entrepreneurs, pitch a first big customer. Inventors, maybe a Lego prototype. (I don't know, what do inventors do?)

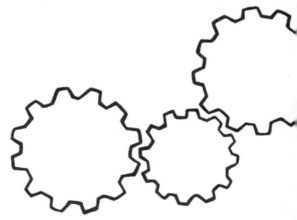

Start First, Plan Second

The single biggest speed bump for stARTists is thinking they need a plan.

Plans are great. You should make plans. Make big plans. Definitely. But don't expect your plans to give you much. As stARTists know, plans are not fun givers; they are boring takers.

Sure, plans bring order to the chaos of starting, but what they give us in structure and certainty they often take away in curiosity, spontaneity, and momentum.

Prolific stARTists keep plans loose and change them along the way. In fact, most say they start first and plan second.

"Plans change the second you start implementing them," says one

serial entrepreneur. "No plan can be relied upon until a thing is underway. When you begin, you'll find things you didn't know to look for: a person who isn't on board, a tech application that's not ready, or, most common, a disconnect with the market."

The more time we spend on the plan and the more sacred we make it, the harder it is to deviate from and keep the process creative.

As we start more, we learn to simply trust the structure of our own starting process.

Some stARTists Never Plan

Some stARTists trust their process so much, they never plan.

Imagine THIS: What if your JOB was to write and perform jokes and songs? Big stARTistic pressure, right? And what if you had to write your jokes, songs, and dances within a brand-new show, WHICH YOU ALSO HAD TO WRITE? Hold on. I'm not done yet.

And . . . what if you had to do it all in front of a full, live audience? No plan, no script.

And wait, I forgot to say that you have to do that over and over again, sometimes EVERY SINGLE NIGHT for weeks. Without repeating yourself.

That's what musical improvisers Ashley Ward, Erica Elam, Nathan Jansen, and Al Samuels do, and we should all have one tiny fraction of their stARTistic bravado.

I learned about musical improvisation from the celebrated company Baby Wants Candy, when my daughter Tess was working on its production crew at the Edinburgh Festival Fringe (a detonation of stARTistic activity every August in Edinburgh, Scotland, that features thousands of shows). Their company sold out every show the six years before our visit, just before the coronavirus pandemic.

We knew somebody running the lights (wink wink), so we got tickets to *Harry Potter and the Goblet of Viagra*. I wouldn't have picked a show by that name, but we didn't know the name of the show until we got there. You see, Baby Wants Candy begins each performance by letting the audience name the show—with titles like (these are actual examples) *How to Slut Shame Your Dragon, The Handmaid's Snail, Sex Toy Story,* and my personal favorite, *Giving Birth in a Walmart.*

The show started like this: A cast member asked the audience to shout out titles, she took the first three ideas, then led a vote by applause. Lights went out for five seconds, then the announcer boomed, "Ladies and gentlemen, Baby Wants Candy presents the opening and sadly also the closing performance of *Harry Potter and the Goblet of Viagra.*" The lights came up, improvisers were in new positions on stage, and the show began. Taking the never-subtle cues of a musical director and the talented Yes bAND, five performers created a story with a plotline and a grand musical finale.

I felt the whole time like I was at a magic show, looking for wires or holograms to explain the unexplainable.

The day after the show, I sat down with some of the improvisers to ask them how they do it. How does every scene, every song, every joke get started? Is it all from scratch, or are there hidden cue cards?

Nope, no cheat sheets or lines fed through earbuds, they told me. Somebody just starts.

"One person just steps forward and says something, and the show is started," says cast member Ashley.

A seasoned improviser, she makes it sound easy. But her executive producer, Al, says Ashley's a pro, and that's her stARTistic conditioning talking.

"A performer must take the title chosen by the audience and make what we call an 'offer,'" says Al. It's a forceful choice—a line of dialogue or lyrics. Their decision starts the show.

For the next forty-five minutes or so, performers seize opportunities to earn laughs and weave a story—musically and comedically.

The musical director is the stARTist in charge. He sets the tempo and musical arc for the show. He listens for places to give musical suggestions, like turning a wacky comeback into a rap, or coaxing a love ballad out of an awkward moment between characters.

In the Baby Wants Candy show *Sarah Palin, The Musical*, a polar bear knocks on the imaginary door of Sarah Palin (Erica with a thick Alaskan accent) and becomes her love interest. Music rises, someone rhymes "fun" with "gun," and before you know it, the polar bear is dead and the entire cast is singing and dancing in unison to the Broadway-style tune "Who Loves Sarah Palin?" (FYI, the musical answer is: "You know! Juno.") That song sets the stage for a string of rapid-fire romantic and political vignettes held together by a cohesive musical score.

Once a musical improv show is underway, it's up to each performer to start their role in it, seemingly by finding a first line that will set them up for success for the rest of the show.

"It doesn't feel that important what you do first. You must just DO ANYTHING . . . right away . . . boldly," says Erica.

"The start is decided in an instant. Then, it's all about what we do with what we did."

"You can't go into it as if there is a right or best line. And you can't second-guess yourself once you put it out there," says Nathan.

And you **can't hesitate**. "If I wait to talk in a scene until I have something really good to say, I will not be in that scene," he says.

"Improv is not about doing it right, it's about DOING IT," says Ashley.

All true, says their boss, Al. "There's no perfect choice. But some choices are better than others. And certainly, there are bad choices—choices that don't move things forward."

"Still, the stakes are incredibly low," says Ashley. "If you try something and it doesn't work, you can try something else in the next minute. What have you lost?"

Musical improv is a master class in taking first action steps. Though they skip the script, improvisers are not without goals and direction. They take the stage with clear objectives—moving scenes forward, creating story lines, and composing songs.

They create magic, not with painstaking plans and rehearsals, but with hundreds of daring acts of stARTistry.

We can learn much from the tenets of musical improvisers:

Just Say "Yes, And"

This is the rule of agreement. Nothing gets started by arguing with yourself or the people you're starting with. Once you have decided to start, say "yes, and" to every step. You're affirming, and moving forward. Second-guessing does not serve your effort. Say "yes, and" to your idea. Say "yes, and" to your first move.

Show, Don't Tell

Take action. Don't TALK about starting. SHOW what you've started. Build a bias for action and make specific, active decisions.

There Are No Mistakes

Ideas aren't good or bad. All choices can be built upon. The best comedy, for example, can come from a seemingly weak line. One player's bad move sets up another's funny response and makes them both look brilliant.

Stay in the Moment

Though creating can seem to be working toward a future result, action happens only in the now. Who are the players? What is the situation? How can you advance with what you have at this moment?

Improvised comedy is mind-blowing. But even stand-up comedians, who plan performances to the detail, will tell you they craft material by starting. They write the beginnings of a joke, then climb on a stage and work it out. They find what lands, what flops, and what gets them to the next funny idea.

A stARTist acts . . .

- *Fast*
- *With curiosity*
- *While we're still afraid*
- *Before we're certain what to do next*
- *Often without plans, supplies, and contingencies*
- *Like we know more than we do*
- *With an expectation that the next step will reveal itself*

TAKE ACTION

(5 TO 20 MINUTES)

1. **Clarify and commit to your idea.** Grab your phone, your journal, and your laptop—if, like most of us, you keep half of your brain there. Stand up and stretch. Move to a good place—a desk-type place where work gets done. Get a glass of water.

If you like art tools, get them—colored pencils, markers, paints, and brushes.

Now go to the idea you started on page 63. It's in your journal. You made a file folder, remember? You have a fun name.

Have you changed your mind to a different idea? Great! Use that one.

2. **Decide your first step.** Look at the ways you said you could start that idea. Remember: "List three ways you could start the project with what you already have."

Examples: a sketch series, collaboration meetings, an outline, a list of partners.

Decide your first action, and take it!

> If your idea is visual, do something visual. (You don't start a painting by writing about it in your calendar.)
>
> If your idea involves writing, write something—not just outlines or schedules. Write a first line or paragraph, a section of dialogue, or an introduction.
>
> If your idea requires bringing people together, call someone, schedule something, or begin the list, roster, or participant profile you envision.

This is exciting! I can almost hear your idea from here, saying, "I thought you'd never ask. Let's DO this!"

3. **Anchor your start.** Invest more action and leave something behind—proof you were here and pressure to move forward. Add next steps to your calendar. Cancel something unimportant to make time for your new project. Draw something, take a picture, or text a friend to say you've begun.

4. **Schedule your next step.** You have started! But maybe you've made it this far before. Tell your brain THIS is the real deal. We do that with action and by committing to restart SOON. Tomorrow? Later today? Put it on the calendar and build in every annoying reminder. This is happening.

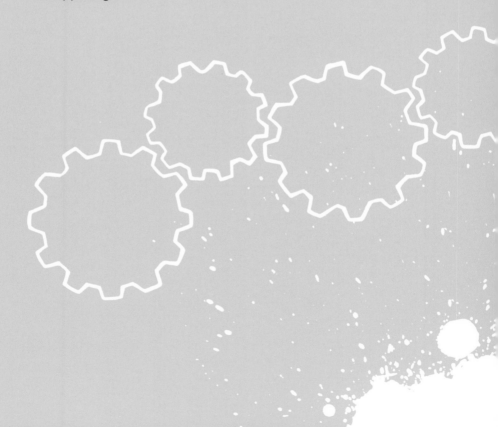

6. OFF To a GOOD stART

How ignition sessions, bumpy beginnings, and a bias for action unleash our best work

Once we've decided to act on an idea, it's good to formalize it—in the most informal way possible. I like to think of it as a warm hug meets a Chinese finger trap. I sit down with the idea and strike a deal: "If you'll show up when I do, I'll do the work."

The idea always shows up.

It might show up tired. It might show up folded and faded like the piece of paper we wrote it on two years ago. Usually, though, our idea will show up like a golden retriever who hasn't seen us all day—crazy goofy excited that we're there . . . waiting to see what we're going to do . . . unconditionally joyful and expectant.

Our job is to do the work. To show up, stay hydrated, and call in help when we need it. To take the first step, and make it count.

You'd probably like some step-by-step instructions and detailed checklists on how to do this. Maybe answers to specific questions.

"How do I *DO* a start?" Where do I sit? How long do I spend? Do I do it alone? When does it count? How should I feel? Who can I tell? Which software is best? Are we using Oxford commas?

Part of the answer came earlier: "Don't overthink it."

If you want to start . . .

. . . **a book**, open a new document on your computer, write some words, and make a decision to open it every day to add words.

. . . **a neighborhood cleanup event**, write an invitation to the neighbors in your address book and invite them. And buy some trash bags.

. . . **a painting**, get a canvas and some paint in the same room and put some of the paint on the canvas. (This, at times, can be unspeakably difficult for some people. We know who we are.)

First steps usually are simple and obvious, depending on the creation.

What you're really craving is a process that makes you feel successful—a tried-and-true feedback loop that you can trust to start easy, often, and with reliable results.

So the second answer to "How do I *DO* a start?" is: **Build a process that works for you.**

This isn't the off-the-rack checklist you were hoping for, but even the perfectionist in you will see the value of crafting your own custom-tailored starting session designed around your ideas, abilities, available space, job demands, biorhythms, and maybe your pet's nap schedule.

Let's start by watching how others do it.

When I ask, "How do you start?" stARTists describe everything from disciplined work sessions to creative free-for-alls.

I met a dress designer who starts a new fashion line by cutting off a few yards of her most expensive fabrics and ripping them into scraps. She pieces together wild garments, frayed edges and all, onto a mannequin. "It gets the creative juices flowing and gets me over being precious with the fabric," she says. Her scrappy starting mannequins become window displays, a trademark of her shop.

She knows her challenge (being protective of her expensive fabric) and her goal (open, unbridled designing). So she's designed a process in response.

To give them the gravitas they deserve, I call initial action events like this "ignition sessions." They run the gamut from two-step rituals like "I put on an apron and dip my brush in the paint" to planned, scheduled, choreographed work sessions. Here are some other examples.

JOSEPHINA, A PROJECT MANAGER, STARTS WITH A SET TIME AND REMOTE PLACE. *"Once a project has a 'go' signal, I set a date and time to begin—usually with a large chunk of time. I start in a conference room, coffee shop, or sometimes the kitchen table— never at my desk."*

TATE, A SONGWRITER, STARTS BY SCHEDULING A SESSION WITH ANOTHER WRITER. *"I've learned that I work best in collaboration, and I schedule two-hour 'writes' with other songwriters. It's a common thing here in Nashville. The day before, I'll read poetry, listen to music, and jot down notes for themes, bridges,* and choruses. I show up with some ideas, but I stay open and build off of what my cowriter brings."

CHRIS, A COMMUNITY ORGANIZER, NEEDS TO START FREE OF DISTRACTIONS: *"I like to have the deck cleared—the office clean, the email inbox cleared, my mom called, and my kids in someone else's care. What I'm creating is sure to add complexity to my life, so I have to feel a sense of control so I won't hold back."*

NICK, A CHEF AND ARTIST, CREATES NEW DISHES BY VISUALIZING THEM AS A WORK OF ART. *"If I want something bright and vegetal, I would see that as green and seek out green ingredients to make it. If I want to do a dish with cauliflower as a main component, I'll look for a contrasting or a complementary color for the sauce. Looking at cookbooks is part of my ritual; they get me excited and remind me of techniques I've forgotten."*

RANIA, A SPEAKER, AUTHOR, AND EXPERT ON INCLUSIVE LEADERSHIP, STARTS BY RESEARCHING. *"Once I have an idea and a decision to make it a talk or an article, my first step is research. I dig around, dive down rabbit holes, and soak in diverse information. I let what I learn direct and motivate me, but never slow me down."*

SADIE, A HUMOR WRITER, LIKES TO START WHERE THE INSPIRATION STRIKES. *"I wrote a piece during my Uber ride home when an editor called asking for a time-sensitive satire. I sometimes go to coffee shops to work on projects for my day job and wind up writing funny pieces inspired by what's going on around me."*

If you want to up your starting game, start finding your how, your where, and maybe your who, then sculpt a go-to process and an ignition session you'll come to trust.

When Is It Started?

You may be asking at this point, just to be clear, "When is something actually STARTED? When does a mere idea graduate to a work-in-progress?"

Here's where it gets tricky, because one person's starting step can be another person's avoidance ploy. Most of creating is a head game, so we must take this head-on by getting honest with ourselves about what is starting and what is something else.

Let's take **talking, researching, and planning**, for example. Are these action steps, or are they regressions back to the "thinking on it" stage? Or is it all just us trying to look smart and feel stARTistic while we procrastinate? (Raises hand: frequently guilty on all counts.)

stARTing IS:

- Talking about it—to get feedback or help
- Planning—to coordinate schedules and put resources in place
- Researching—to find inspiration and clarity

sTARTing IS NOT

- Talking about it—to impress people with your idea
- Planning—for the purpose of delaying until everything is perfect and foolproof
- Researching—just to be sure that no one's done this before or to find other reasons why your idea is not worth doing . . . because it costs too much . . . or because it's too big to finish on your lunch hour

Action feels like action, not avoidance.

If we spend a lot of time with an idea, and it's no closer to being real than the day we imagined it, then we're not off to a good start.

Here's how self-aware stARTists answer the question "How do you know you've made a good start?"

"I know it's a good start when the next several steps are clear and obvious." —SERIAL STARTIST

"A good starting session is one that I leave knowing it's a project I'll invest in—that I've wrangled enough details to convince others it's a worthy idea." —REAL ESTATE DEVELOPER

"My start—the first time I sit down to build a tour—must be foundational. I need to finish an outline of location, schedule, target market, etc., to have a solid base to build from." —TOUR DESIGNER AND TRAVEL PLANNER

"I write as much as I can in the first sitting, until I'm exhausted and almost hate the idea. It's like uncorking the bottle. I feel started, because I know the next sitting will have surprises." —FICTION WRITER

"For big beginnings, I need some ceremony. Though I may have played with ideas for weeks, I call it started only once I've named it, made a notebook and files, and bought a new project coffee cup (my little ritual)." —PLAYWRIGHT, SCREENWRITER, AND AUTHOR

"I put enough definition to the idea that I can explain it to my wife and kids. Then it's started." —CORPORATE SPEAKER AND TRAINER

"An idea is launched when I put enough in writing that I can go back to it later and know next steps, even after a break of weeks or months." —BUSINESS STRATEGIST

"Honestly, most of my inventions don't have crisp beginnings. Ideas come when I'm tinkering or fixing something. Then I usually just go with it—start and maybe finish that day." —MECHANICAL ENGINEER AND INVENTOR

Learn what makes you feel truly started.
Talk to other stARTists and practice, practice, practice.

Start on Demand

"Be careful what you wish for," a young friend told me after starting his new job as an advertising writer. "Being creative on demand every day is not the same as making your own stuff on your own timetable."

After a little time on the job, his laments ceased. He had built skills that made it easy to face the blank page, even at someone else's direction. He had turned pro.

This topic intrigued researcher Dennis Greene. How do people create on demand? Isn't inspiration something that visits on its own schedule? In hundreds of in-depth interviews and surveys, Greene studied serial creators to find out how they do it, to find commonalities we can learn from.

Greene found good news—that consistently creative people who start and restart projects and solve problems on demand have things in common. Their processes almost always include:

1. A ritual

2. A conscious shift to a state of contemplation

3. Thought-out questions to direct the process

We've talked about purposeful thinking and using questions through the starting process in earlier chapters. Adding ritual ties the process together with a bow.

Rituals run the gamut from a morning walk, which Greene's study found to be by far the most common ritual of creatives, to silly, irrational behaviors like turning off and on lights, or clapping hands a certain number of times.

Walking and other exercise have their own collections of healthy benefits, of course. So much, in fact, that walks could be a prescribed precursor to every creative session. But mounting research shows that any ritual, even a silly one, sets us up for creative success.

Performing a ritual of our own can give us a sense of control over our thoughts, feelings, and behaviors. Research shows that rituals improve focus, concentration, attention, and confidence, and they reduce anxiety. They regulate aspects of our performance, helping us, for example, tolerate frustration and not see it as failure.

If you know your ritual, embrace it. If you don't have one, start paying attention. Maybe you'll see that singing that song to your ficus plant before you put your coffee in your favorite *Star Wars* cup is part of getting your gears turning.

But heads up, Greene says. "Rituals are only as strong as we make them. The most confident creators activate their rituals daily."

Create every day? I'm here for that!

Okay then, to wrap up: All starts are good. Good starts are better. I'm glad we agree.

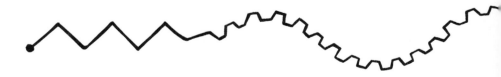

And, just to be clear, you can start acting on your idea anywhere, anytime, with no plans or fanfare or virtual assistants. You heard that, right? Just making sure.

I think I also said that if you want to start more, better, easier, and with more control to do your best work, then you may want to create your own special, custom-fitted, everything-your-stARTistic-heart-desires starting process that works for you. Here's how:

1. **SCHEDULE AND DESIGN YOUR STARTING SESSION.** Find or make a place that tells your subconscious "ignition happens here." Include whatever people, preparation, and inspiration you need, and build your session to make you feel truly started.

2. **KNOW YOUR RITUAL, OR BUILD ONE.** Call forth your muses. Take a walk or a bike ride. Make preparations: get a glass of water, line up your pencils, sniff some eucalyptus. Ignite your work by consciously shifting your thinking to a single first step.

3. **BRING A QUESTION.** Direct your thinking with a question, such as . . .

   - What is the best first step?
   - What will get the idea traction and momentum?
   - What will move this from an idea to a work-in-progress?
   - What is one thing I can do to _____?
   - What is asking to be solved by my idea? How can I begin solving it fastest?
   - What can I do to engage people/energy/ideas ASAP?

4. **RECORD AND REWARD.** Chronicle your work in writing, video, sound recording, drawing, etc. If the work IS the chronicle, like writing an article, do something more to record it. Take a picture of the first page on your computer, make a playful entry in your journal, or record yourself hitting "save." Build in goofy treats and rewards to keep you coming back.

Bump into Things

Once you begin them, novels and companies are similar stARTistic adventures. You don't know your customers or characters until they present themselves, and it's in trying to serve them that the magic happens. All you can do is start anew with each encounter—each page, each product, each plot twist.

Novelist E. L. Doctorow said, "Writing a novel is like driving a car at night. You can see only as far as your headlights, but you can make the whole trip that way."

What a relief. We don't have to see as far ahead as we think we do. We just need to see what's right in front of us.

Honestly, creating anything is like driving at night. We start wherever we can see. We turn on the brights, if we can. We fix our sights on the farthest point, and we step on the gas. When we get to the thing we fixed our sights on, that's our new starting place.

Often, when moving quickly in and out of starting stages, toward ideas and discoveries, we don't know where to fix our sights. It's like we're off the road in bumper cars.

That's not a bad thing.

We bump into new friends and collaborators, new ideas, and new methods. We bump into things that were right under our noses and things we forgot to consider when we were turning our sizzling idea into an overcooked plan.

When we take action, we bump into answers. More important, we bump into questions.

"It's impossible to ask all the right questions when you're in planning mode," says one serial business stARTist. "Only real life gives you real problems. And problems fuel innovation."

A question on the page—on a plan, on a schedule, on a budget— is way different than a question in the moment. I learned this while bumping around with my lacy things.

Several years after I sold my PR business and got some art and writing out of my system, I took a trip to my favorite city, Paris. Somewhere between the designer boutiques, the flea markets, and the seedy fabric district of Montmartre, I got the idea for my next business: a fashion accessories company. We would specialize in high-end bridal garters made of vintage French lace and the finest silk ribbon. Because if there is a time when a woman should have a scrumptious piece of French lace no matter what the cost, and if there is a time when rich Aunt Eliza wants to show off by buying a classy gift no matter what the cost, it's for a wedding.

I took swift action. I sewed a few samples, researched the competition in bridal stores and on Etsy, and studied pricing. I checked out market shows and the distribution channels of the wedding industry. And I showed my samples to anyone who would look.

Along the way, I bumped into sourcing questions. How will I get enough vintage lace? Where do I source high-quality ribbon on par with the quality of the lace? How much do I have to buy at a time to get a good price?

I bumped into questions about the bridal category: What can a bride do with a $300 garter after she wears it for one special day? How much must I spend on packaging? How can I make it valuable past the wedding day?

I thought I had bumped into my first big customer when a high-end boutique offered to buy all my samples . . . until she measured my garters. "Sorry. My girls have bigger thighs. I can't sell this many small ones," the proprietress said. Oops. I had made equal numbers of small, medium, and large samples, based on no research at all. That's how I learned that sizing and inventory decisions require knowing your customers.

More disappointment came when I learned from a wedding planner that the tradition of brides throwing garters is on the decline. Bummer. Glad I asked!

Undeterred, I pivoted. I refashioned some garter designs into everyday accessories like chokers, wrist cuffs, and hair ornaments, to make a line of fancy, funky nonbridal accessories.

By hauling off and making prototypes and visiting vendors, I bumped into answers to questions I didn't know to ask.

Questions are the gifts action gives us.

A question in action is a question in context. It's answered by reality, not hunch or hypothesis. It leads straight to the next better question.

Here are some questions best answered once you get started:

What could go right?

What could go wrong?

What does success look like?

How does it feel to do this?

Who cares?

Who else would like this?

Do I need more research?

Should I throw away my research?

Can I stay up this late every night?

Who should I tell?

Whose help do I really need?

Would this product work for dogs?

Can I do this while I sleep?

Should I let sleeping dogs lie?

Would sleeping dogs make this more fun?

Is this easier than riding a bike?

Can I do this while riding a bike?

Would this be better in the rain?

Would more people like this if I showed it to them on Thursday?

How long will this keep at room temperature?

Can I do this every day?

What if I double this?

What if I triple that?

What if? What if? What if?

Talking to shopkeepers and garment makers, I learned that if I didn't want to sell my wares online or personally walk the streets, I needed a showroom in New York. So off I went to the Big Apple to buy ribbon and to interview showrooms. As a first-timer with no introduction, I could only get appointments with two showrooms. (Even though designers PAY showrooms 10 to 15 percent, the good showrooms are selective about who they take on to fill their limited slots.)

One was all I needed, and I struck gold in the first appointment. It wasn't glamorous.

I taxied to the address on 23rd Street in Manhattan, a ten-story brick building. I rang the old beat-up doorbell, and someone buzzed me in and directed me to the fifth floor. A fashionable fortyish woman met me at the door and walked me through the cramped aisles of showcases filled with jewelry and fashion accessories. We settled at a small table in the corner of the room where I unpacked my proto-types and made my pitch.

She was nice. Receptive. She picked up each piece to examine it closely. My hopeful designer heart soared when she said things like, "Yes, these are fresh." And, "I can see these in Barneys." She said her showroom sold to some of the most prestigious, high-end retailers in the world, and she thought my pieces would stack up. Then, she walked me around the showroom to see the other lines they represented.

It became clear that SHE was now selling ME. I was IN. We sat back down and she ticked through the terms, costs, and showroom fees. The costs she quoted didn't surprise me. I had done my home-work. But then, she said something that may be so implied in the fashion world that it escaped my research: "You have time to get this collection in for the spring," she said. "What do you have in mind for the fall?"

Wait. Fall? Another collection by FALL? This collection took me a year to pull together. And I wasn't sure how I was going to ramp up manufacturing for it yet. Would I need a new collection every season? This was sounding like a full-time start-up, which means an eighty-hour-a-week job. I didn't want one of those. This was my "lifestyle" business—the fun thing I was doing after selling the hard thing.

I knew in my gut from that meeting that this was not what I wanted, but I didn't close the door right away. I visited with some successful designers and fashion creators to check out my hunches— people who wouldn't have made time for me if I wasn't in conversations with that showroom.

They confirmed my fears . . . that fashion manufacturing is all-consuming work. It's not a sideline.

Oh, boy, it was difficult, but I walked away from the showroom deal. I went back home and sold my small stock of merchandise to boutiques and online retailers. I made back my investment and a little profit. I held on to some wedding garters for my daughters and a few favorite accessories for myself.

I don't know how I would have learned what I did about start-ing a fashion business without taking action . . . without hauling off and sewing. Only when I had prototypes could I bump around on the fringes of an industry I didn't know to learn what was really required.

Stories like this usually end in more exciting, lucrative ways than mine did. Entrepreneurs start with one product and bump into a better one. They start solving a small problem and bump into a bigger one. And they bump into lessons they could not have learned any other way.

I'm telling you a story of "losing" instead of "winning" to drive home the point. I'm grateful for what I bumped into—it was exactly what I needed. I got affirmation for my creations, and happened onto introspection I needed: I liked designing. I liked making things. But I didn't want to start a manufacturing business at age fifty.

I whined into my journal and sorted my thoughts. I engaged a gallery to sell my artwork and started a tiny tour company. What I learned about French lace and fashion enriches my closet and inspires my art. No regrets.

When we act on our ideas, we bump into our own creative clarity.

And, we bump into some stop signs. When we act on our ideas, we eventually bump into their finishes. Sadly, they're not always the finishes we planned.

Not all ideas deserve our everything. Not all ideas have the potential we imagine.

Not all ideas should be executed until the bitter finish.

Spotting the true stop signs and potential of our ideas gets easier with practice. And the things we bump into when we take action give us three huge consolation prizes:

- **We learn.** Yes, we learn how to recognize a failed course of action and to cut our losses, which are important skills. That's just the beginning. When we're in the thick of it—in motion, in problem-solving, how-can-we-do-this mode—we learn things we don't know we need to know, things a book or class can never teach.

- **We save time.** Ideas take up brain space and time, even when we're just sitting around with them. Clearing out one idea makes room for the next, better one.

- **We sidestep regret.** No doubt about it, when we take the risk of investing in our ideas, we are happier with ourselves. Daniel Pink, author of *The Power of Regret*, says people who took a risk and failed had many fewer regrets than people who never took a risk at all. "When we act, we know what happened next," says Pink. "But when we don't . . . we can only speculate how events would have unfolded. The consequences of actions are specific, concrete and limited. The consequences of inaction are general, abstract and unbounded."

Bumping into Bubble Wrap

Bubble wrap never had a place on anyone's "Things to Start" list. Two designers bumped into the idea when they set out to make textured wallpaper.

Teflon was invented in the 1930s by a twenty-seven-year-old trying to create a nontoxic refrigerant. Years later, Marion Trozzolo put it on frying pans.

Post-Its started as a high-strength glue.

Play-Doh started as wallpaper cleaner.

The Slinky was invented when a mechanical engineer, designing a device to secure cargo on ships, spilled coiled wires on the floor. He saw them tumble playfully, end over end. Next stop, toy shop!

Coca-Cola began as a treatment for morphine addiction, headaches, and anxiety.

Listerine got its start as a cure for gonorrhea.

Oops, we've taken a gritty turn here. You get the picture. When we set an idea in motion, we start a loopy, never-ending coil of possibilities.

Start something, bump into something else.

Action Teaches

What have you learned by taking quick action on your ideas?

Here are responses from other stARTists:

Twenty people are too many for a book club.

More can go wrong than I thought.

The potential is bigger than I thought.

This would look better in green.

Dogs won't like this, but cats will.

You can't substitute kosher salt for table salt.

If people read the instructions, they're less likely to return this.

Most people don't read the instructions.

My boss knows more than I gave him credit for.

Remote-control vacuum cleaners give people the creeps.

Invoicing takes more time than you think.

Unmonitored Zoom breakout rooms don't work for high school students.

Lawyers actually do serve a purpose.

My mom was right about some things.

It really does have to look good to taste good.

Timing is not everything, but it's pretty important.

Let your gut guide you. But your gut won't have anything to work with if you stay in the same place. Move. Act. Bump into things.

A Bias for Action

Once ideas are rolling, we have to seize every chance to move them along. This is where a bias for action drives better work and creativity.

To keep restarts firing, I like to use the Five-Second Rule.

It's not the rule where if food falls on the floor you have to eat it within five seconds; it's the idea by celebrated author and podcast host Mel Robbins, who says, "If you have an impulse to act on a goal, you must physically move within five seconds or your brain will kill the idea." She suggests that once you know what you need to do, you count backward: 5 . . . 4 . . . 3 . . . 2 . . . 1 . . . ACTION. Counting and acting immediately, she says, silences the mind and prevents us from talking ourselves out of action and into procrastination. And, it makes a psychological intervention to help override anxiety while reinforcing a habit of courage and movement.

I'm pretty quick to the Batmobile when starting big new things, but day to day, the Five-Second Rule helps me . . .

1. Write down ideas before I forget them, in my journal.

2. Pick up the phone before I think of reasons not to call someone.

3. Ask for a favor before I lose my nerve.

4. Set up supplies for an art project, so it's ready when I am.

5. Schedule a consult or collaboration with a new person, before I convince myself it won't be worth the time—it's ALWAYS worth the time.

6. Sketch or search for a visual reference, while the notion is fresh.

7. Schedule a starting session.

8. Make new people connections.

Give Your Idea a Fair Fight

Our hesitation habits cost ideas their lives.

Behavioral scientists tell us that when we weigh decisions, we tend to focus more on what we have to *lose* than what we stand to *gain*. It's a well-studied phenomenon called *loss aversion*. We're wired to worry more about losing a dollar than we delight in gaining a dollar. We dread the high school bully making fun of us more than we look forward to the joy of busting our best moves in the high school talent show. We tip our decisions toward dodging what we don't want rather than chasing what we do.

The good news is, we can use this.

By taking swift action, we shift the equation. By starting fast, before we focus on what we could lose, we make our idea something we don't want to lose. **When we invest in it—with time, thought, energy, resources—our idea gains advantage.** Our brain must then choose between losing the now-real progress on our idea and the imaginary scaredy-cat stuff we come up with to keep us in our comfort zone.

Give your idea a fair fight. Invest with action.

A Year of Starting Anything

I wondered whether I could build my bias for action—to act on bigger ideas, and to be creative on demand with ideas I didn't originate. So I declared my year of saying "start"—to my own ideas, and to ideas that seemed to have my name on them.

My commitment was this: If an idea comes my way that makes sense for me, I will quickly say, "I'll start," and take action.

And though I start things all the time, that year I actually blew my own mind.

- I gave my first comedy performance.
- I created a sold-out comedy show.
- I wrote my first song.
- I staged four fundraising parties, including a 350-person gala.
- I hired a choreographer and produced a dance program (at the gala).
- I made a set of human-size dog costumes (see above, dance program).
- I made thirty-four art pieces.
- I started a zany garden artscape.
- I started a tree-planting project.
- I started three articles and several sections of this book.
- I started an Instagram account.

Most were one-time projects for me—like making dog costumes for dancers. I wouldn't trade that one for anything.

Other starts, like the tree-planting project, are a part of my life now. I'm on a mission to plant a thousand trees before I die, and yes, I will bore you to tears with my tree hugging.

The comedy show, *Ladies Laugh Lounge*, wins the prize for the most out-of-my-comfort-zone project, so I should tell you about that one.

A few weeks before Mother's Day, my then-twenty-five-year-old daughter, Taylor Kay Phillips, a comedy writer in New York, invited me to do a show with her humor writing group. Seven women in the group had all invited their moms to do the Mother's Day show at a club in Brooklyn.

I'm not a comedian or a performer, and though I like to find the snark and humor in everything, this was not my jam.

But Taylor assured me I was up to it. "It's just comedy writers reading their pieces, Mom. Just write something funny. You'll be great. You said this was your year of starting new things."

Whoa, had I said that out loud?

This was the same kid who cast me in her backyard play and told me to publish my first book, so guess how many choices I had. I said "yes" on the spot and found a YouTube video for stage fright.

Over the next two weeks, I wrote an article I thought was funny, and flew to New York to meet up with both my daughters for Mother's Day. When Tess arrived from Chicago, we met at the hotel and I read the piece to her. She didn't gut laugh, but she was affirming. When

Taylor showed up, we met her in the lobby bar. I read my piece again, expecting to receive what every performer should get from a director the day before a show: light edits and gushing accolades.

If memory serves, her exact words were, "Okay, this is funny, Mom, but this is not what we're doing. You need to rewrite this."

She also chose that moment to tell me I was the only mother who had said "yes" to being in the show. I would be the only performer over age thirty-five, besides the featured guest, Emily Flake, a hilarious writer for the *New Yorker*, in her early forties.

So, as you can imagine, confidence was oozing from my pores when I stepped into that hip club, packed to the gills with millennials, with an article I'd rewritten two hours before.

At the front of the room was a tiny unintimidating stage, but on the wall beside it was a big-screen TV, which no one could figure out how to turn off. That wasn't the worst part. Showing onscreen was the next-to-the-last episode of *Game of Thrones*, and the club owner didn't want to unplug it for fear they wouldn't be able to turn it on again, because immediately following our performance was a *Game of Thrones* finale watch party. If ever there was a moment I did not want to finish what I had started, this was it, my friends.

Taylor was the emcee, and when my time came, she introduced me with all the necessary credentials. "You guys, it's my MOM!"

In that instant, it became the perfect evening.

The other performers had read from their tiny phones with their perfect vision, but I stepped proudly onto the stage with my iPad and 20-point type.

There were shoulder pad jokes that didn't land and pop culture references that missed the millennial mark, but mostly people laughed in all the right places, and I felt like a rock star. For someone who writes only for the written page, the audience feedback was exhilarating.

I felt so good about the show that I did what all middle-aged women do when we're proud of ourselves. I posted about it on Facebook.

Comments popped on immediately. "Becky, show us the piece!" "Becky, where's the video?" "Becky, do a show in Kansas City!"

And, there it was, happening again. An idea was waving its smart-alecky hand at me. I could not run. I could not hide. But also, I was kind of liking this.

Before I logged out of Facebook, I had said "yes" to producing a local women's comedy reading show. I messaged a local humor writer, Jen Mann, and asked her to join in and help me find more funny women. I didn't know it at the time, but Jen was in a year of saying "yes" to invitations and opportunities, so she was on board. The comedy muses were smiling on us.

I took action, seat-of-the-pants:

- I canvassed the city for venues and chose the easy option—a new comedy club close to my house.
- I brainstormed with friends and named the show *Ladies Laugh Lounge*. I wasn't crazy about the name, but it made me giggle when I paired it with a vintage painting of a woman fanning herself on a chaise lounge.

- I wrote "Ladies Laugh Lounge" in Sharpie on a piece of masking tape, and stuck it to a grainy printout of the painting to make a logo for the show. The toner needed to be changed in my printer, but it would have slowed me down. The amateurish, kitschy look turned out to be perfect.

- I invited people using a Facebook Event and a few personal emails.

- I scouted in comedy clubs for women to fill out and diversify the show.

The victories were delicious and important:

- **THE SHOW SOLD OUT.** People squeezed in—some sat at tables with strangers, some sat at the club lobby bar to listen through the sound system, and some were turned away at the door.

- **PEOPLE GOT PAID.** I didn't know how much to pay performers, so I did what seemed fair: I split proceeds equally. For some, it was the first time they had ever been paid to perform, and for experienced comedians, it was one of the biggest paychecks of their careers. (Comedy has a messed-up economic model.)

- **MY MOM CAME**, even after my warning that things might get R-rated. I said "orgasm" in front of her for the first time, so now that's out of the way.

BUILD YOUR BIAS FOR ACTION

(20 TO 60 MINUTES)

1. **Build on your decision formula.** Revisit your deciding rules from page 107 and add rules to shift your bias toward action.

For small actions: List specific times you'll use the Five-Second Rule.

Examples:

- Asking for help
- Recording/filing an idea
- Writing a note
- Scheduling action
- Finding a contact

For big starts: Set a goal or time frame to start ideas.

Examples: I will . . .

- Take action on any idea that builds my public speaking skills.
- Choose one idea each week and take action on it.
- Meet with a stARTist friend once a month for the next year and let them choose an idea for me to take action on that day/week.
- Say "yes" to anyone who asks to collaborate on an idea.
- Set aside an hour a week for ideas on my list.
- Start ten ideas from my list this year.

2. **Chronicle your fast-action victories.** Make a place in your journal to write about the times you seized the moment to build your bias for action. How did it feel, and what did you learn? Celebrating the results of action builds the habit and cuts anxiety for future action.

7. ONCE UPON a RestART

A tale of dirty laundry shows us how to stop, restart, and rewrite the rules

My husband and I used to go to bookstores on date night. On nearly every visit, scanning the shelves, he would say, "Can you believe there are all these books in the world and we didn't write any of them?"

Then I would say, "Yes, I *can* believe it. We've been busy. Stop ruining date night."

Many of us romanticize the idea of being an author. In fact, research says that 80 to 90 percent of Americans want to write a book sometime in their lives. It's by far the most popular answer when I ask people, "What do you want to make that you have not started?"

I have my doubts as to whether that many people really want to *write* a book. I think most of us just want to *have* a book *written by us*. Or we just want the street cred of being an "author." These are three very different things, and I'm okay with all of them.

As for me, after writing as a mercenary in an agency for more than a decade, I wanted all of it. I wanted to write a book. I wanted to wear tweed jackets while I toiled in coffee shops, I wanted to hang around other authors, and I most certainly wanted a book to hold in my hand that had my name on the cover. Of course, I wanted it to be fast and easy.

Even though I had never written fiction or taken a fiction class, I was certain the great American novel was inside me, and that it would pop out just as soon as I could carve out a little free time. So when I sold my PR firm and took some time off to decide what to do with the rest of my life, I got a tweed jacket and declared the time arrived.

I found a coffee shop where no one knew me and started writing. I struggled. I restarted. I took a webinar on character development and started again. Somewhere on a floppy disc in a Rubbermaid storage bin are four bad first chapters of novels the world can live without.

Then one date night in the bookstore, scanning shelves of books that I hadn't written, I ran across *No Plot? No Problem*, by Chris Baty. It's a tiny, tidy volume with a quick, clear message: "Sit down and write your novel, start to finish. You have thirty days." In a comforting, here-take-my-hand tone, Baty says, "Don't worry about plots or perfection. Write 2,000 words a day. No problem." Then he offers chapter-by-chapter pep talks for the journey.

Baty's secret formula is two simple rules: no research and no back reading.

When you're writing a novel, you're making up a story, so just make it up with your own experience, he says. Don't go off researching the actual color of Cleopatra's favorite earrings to use in an argument between your main character and a bus driver. And when you're on chapter 10 and you can't remember why your main character knew so much about Cleopatra, don't stop writing to hunt through the first three chapters for the passing reference to her college days.

Without these rabbit holes to fall into, you just start. Every time you sit down to write, you have everything you need. Then you start again tomorrow, right where you left off.

These two rules save novice book writers from themselves, from our tendencies to try too hard and to do things too well. They rescue us from **two time-gobblers that take energy out of starting: procrastinating by proofing, and paralysis by analysis.**

The *No Plot? No Problem* model gives just enough deadlines to keep the pressure on—it's hard to make the 50,000-word writing goal if you skip writing for more than a day or two. This allows new writers to quickly build a mini habit. We get to start writing joyfully every day. No preplanning, no overthinking. And no looking back at what we did yesterday to discourage ourselves.

Well, I did it. I wrote a 50,000-word book in a month by writing about 2,000 words a day.

I titled my debut book *An Elm Tree in Paris*. It's the story of a forty-year-old Kansas woman named Lola who discovers she's the illegitimate love child of a French aristocrat and a Moulin Rouge dancer. It becomes a mystery when Lola goes to Paris in search of her rich deadbeat dad and her bohemian French mother and happens onto a three-generation family conspiracy. A shallow love story with an art heist subplot, it's set in the majesty of the world's most beautiful city, so what's not to love? Remember, I had to write without researching, so I used only artists I knew reliable details about, like Salvador Dalí and Pablo Picasso. And all the action happened on iconic Paris streets or at well-known tourist attractions.

An Elm Tree in Paris was what kind editors would call "inconsistent"; it had its moments, though not enough of them. But I call it a success, because, while it didn't start a breakout fiction career, it started much more than one finished book. It started . . .

1.   A strong daily writing habit.

2.   A fun, enduring schtick with friends. (The few people who read the book like to remind me of a few huge plot holes, some weird characters who changed names between chapters, and the guy who went to the bathroom in Spain and never came back.)

3.   An alter ego based on the main character, Lola, who has become my muse and happiness barometer, and whose name I give the barista when I don't want to hear "Becky" called out in a crowded coffee shop.

4.   A lifestyle tour business called Travels with Lola, which leads tours of small groups through Paris and southern France. Tours are themed with a fun, fictional backstory so travelers see France through the eyes of Lola, who, in search of her bohemian mother and aristocratic father, meanders curiously through corners of Paris not frequented by tourists. A tour with Lola has lots of cafés and people-watching, and hardly any waiting in lines.

It turns out, maybe I'm not a natural fiction writer. But I am a writer. And until I started writing every day, I wasn't sure.

Rewrite Your Rules

When you think about it, "no back reading and no research" is sort of *rule breaking* disguised as *rule making*. I call them "unruly reminders," because they help us sidestep rules that are only required by the finish—to get creative momentum going.

Writers seem to know better than most that the best rules are about reducing requirements.

Better creativity is about peeling off the pressure, not piling it on.

Writer's writer Anne Lamott offers two popular depressurizing rules to get to our best writing:

- Short assignments
- God-awful first drafts

In her book *Bird by Bird*, she explains how short assignments keep our expectations compact and reward us with mini-finishes.

God-awful first drafts give us permission to start with the first thing that comes out. They allow us to be gen-

tle with ourselves. Most of all, this permission slip reminds us that we work in drafts . . . in layers.

A very bad first draft is a very good first step.

Stephen King, author of so many books he won't even commit to a number (somewhere over sixty), in his book *On Writing,* writes a love letter to vocabulary, style, usage, and language. But when he talks about first drafts and getting started, he gives us the rewritten rule we've all been waiting for: "Don't obsess about grammar."

I expand this to: "Don't obsess about punctuation, spelling, word choice, or anything that gets in the way of getting your ideas laid down. All that can be fussed over later, hopefully by someone else."

Unruly reminders get us in position to start—easily and eagerly. They free us to act on our ideas, not on the rules that separate us from them.

If you're *not* a writer, if you're a mannequin designer or a landscape architect or an anti-kale activist, think about what rule-breaking rules might free up your next start. Writing rules transfer easily to most creative starts:

Short assignments. We all need to feel a sense of progress. Chunking up our starts keeps us in the moment and free from overwhelm.

No backtracking or retracing steps. No looking at yesterday's work if it snags you in the weeds. Keep momentum facing forward.

Don't be stalled by research. Let me make sure I say this right, because research is a magical, necessary stage of creating. It's a place where good ideas are born and bad ideas are put out of their misery. In fact, research is a first action step for many creations, and part of many a creative ritual. However, depending on what we're creating, research can be self-sabotage. Focused investigation takes us to a different part of our brain, out of the flow of lateral thinking, away from creativity. Get to know the difference. Use research to help you build on your ideas, not entangle them.

God-awful first drafts. The first pass at something is not proof or disproof of its potential. It's simply a necessary step to get the ball rolling. Get it down.

Don't obsess about details (like grammar). The time for precision is not in the beginning, when your idea is coming into being. Focus first on creation, not correctness.

You may not think of them as rules, but adages, maxims, and rules of thumb like "Don't start more than you can finish" or "Better safe than sorry" can hold powerful sway over us. Find or design the rules that unleash your most creative work.

Shortened Stories

You're now reading my sixth book.

My first is the bad first draft of the novel I just told you about. Fun fact: It's the only one of my books that is not published. If I haven't said it before, you're welcome for that.

My second, third, and fourth books are, let's just say, *compact* volumes, which I wrote on a beach trip with girlfriends. Their titles:

- *I Want to Write a Book*
- *How to Have More Author Friends*
- *The Day God Invented Cheese*

The trick to **finishing** these books was to keep them short—fifty words or less. The trick to **publishing** them was to bind them myself and print only one copy. (And in case you're wondering, the trick to having more author friends is making your friends write books.)

Imagine a brightly colored 3-by-4-inch (7.6-by-10-centimeter) book of eight pages bound at the spine with a staple, or a few funky stitches of string. *You can publish your own book with the fast-track "Become an Author" exercise on page 170. Get excited!*

None of my first four books sold a single copy.

However, my fifth book is a bestseller. *Do Your Laundry or You'll Die Alone: Advice Your Mom Would Give If She Thought You Were Listening* is a sassy gift book in its second edition and its eighth printing. It's won some nice acclaim, and it's making a little money. Which is funny, because out of all of my books, it's the only one I didn't actually start.

What I mean is, I didn't start it as a *book*. I started a journal entry . . . on a bad day.

It was a string of bad days, actually.

You see, by the time my daughters were seventeen and fourteen, my mom work seemed pretty much done. They could dress themselves, their eye-rolling skills were nearly perfect, and one of them was driving. I was invisible, as nature intended, but also constantly in their way.

And so it was the first morning of my older daughter Taylor's senior year of high school, sitting in the quiet house about to get quieter, that I began journaling about the terror that strikes every parent as their kids fly the nest: the fear my kid had missed everything I said. Watching her stress out about college applications, unhappy in what should have been her happiest year, and seemingly incapable of completing a load of laundry, I decided I had failed at parenting. Time had slipped through my fingers, and I had not taught my daughter what she needed to know. So I began a list—a too-late list of things I thought my kid needed to know to be a good human, no matter which college she got into.

Through the year, when something she did without looking up from her phone made me feel like a bad mom, I went to my journal. It became a system for survival. Over time, it became more than a list, and more than just the bad stuff. It turned into mini essays, memory captures, and notes to self to remind me how things actually turn out okay. And it was my therapy, slowly walking me to a place of acceptance, that the human I started eighteen years ago was not a finished project, and that I needed to put my stARTistic energies elsewhere.

We lived through the year. Barely. And when she moved into her dorm, I typed up the fifty-some pages of my journal and emailed them with a subject line I hoped would make it through the noise of her freshman inbox: *Do your laundry or you'll die alone.*

Days later, Taylor wrote back. "Mom, this email is funny. My roommates think so, too. You should make it into a book. You should put your art in it and have it done by the time Tess graduates from high school next year."

One thing you realize when your kids stop listening to you is that the only means you have of teaching them is by your example. So when Taylor, who wanted to be a writer, challenged me to put my writing out into the world, I had exactly zero choices in the matter.

So I started again. I started looking at what I had written with new eyes. Which points were universal, and which were inside family jokes? How snarky is too snarky? I began thinking and adding, and showing up to start again and again.

A thousand times, I did things that some might call quitting. But they were just pauses . . . part of creating.

I waited too long to look into the process of publishing, because when I did, I learned it takes months to get an agent, who will take months to secure a publisher, who will take more than a year to get the book in print. Yikes. My deadline of Tess's graduation was less than a year away.

I decided to self-publish. "Serious" authors told me it was a cop-out, that the book wouldn't sell or be respected unless it had a mainstream publisher. Even as the internet was creating breakout success stories with self-publishing formats, author friends told me that a book I published myself was not a "real" book. But I had no choice. I was out of time.

Having run a marketing firm, I knew how to make a printed product look top-notch. It became a challenge. I resolved that my book would be a work of art, of quality exceeding the most respected publishers. I got a bid from a printer friend, then I skipped over to my computer and started a publishing company.

I didn't need employees or a new address. I just needed to contract some services and pay a lawyer to file some stuff. (There's always a lawyer.)

My publishing company did for my little book what the big publishing houses do for the big books. It found an editor and proofreaders, hired a designer for the cover layout and page design, registered the book with the Library of Congress, and got an ISBN number. It contracted a printer, a warehouse, and a distribution house, so I didn't have to sell books out of the trunk of my car, and so my husband could see them on the bookstore shelf on date night.

We interrupt this long story to call out a key point, which you might have missed buried in the compelling saga of motherly love: Everything my publishing company did, YOU, or ANY stARTist, can do on the internet. It's a huge pain in the @$$, and you may not choose it; you may have to save your nickels or do a GoFundMe, but you do not need to be selected, or anointed, or invited for tea.

I published the first edition of *Do Your Laundry or You'll Die Alone* in the nick of time for Tess's graduation in May.

I gave books to my daughter and her friends on their graduation day. I gave books to grieving empty-nesting mom friends to help them hug/nag their launching children. I had a book with my name on it and my words in it. More important, my heart was in it.

In no small way, that book had saved me. Starting the day of my firstborn's senior year, and finishing the day my younger daughter turned me into an empty nester, the creation pulled me along, gently, to my most dreaded restarting place.

I didn't start out to save myself. I didn't even start out to write a book. I just started writing one day about what was on my mind.

Permission to Pause

I don't know you, but I know you've started and finished thousands of things. And along the way, you've made tens of thousands of pauses or stops. You did not quit. You simply stopped. You disengaged. You paused.

You didn't do anything wrong.

Setting projects aside is fine. Running out of time is fine. Stopping is fine.

When we create a lot, we build faith in the creative process. We learn that it's a system of layers and messes and taking breaks, a process where nothing is wasted, not even the breaks.

When we stop, we stop.

A stARTist may call a break by many names, like "rest" or "recess" or "time-out." They certainly will NOT call it "quit" or "fail."

The way stARTists grow is by learning to make our stops count. We decide where to stop and how we'll restart. We decide how to show up again for our creation and what we will do first.

If we're starting a painting, maybe we leave a sticky note saying, "Start mixing blue for here." If we're writing a novel, maybe we leave a plot note at the top of the page saying, "Dr. StrangeGlove is preparing dinner for his new assistant. She likes risotto." Authors often use this technique to take the pressure off the next work session. Educators, inventors, business innovators, and artists employ versions of their own.

As we stop for the day or the week, we might give our brain an assignment—ask it a question, or tell it to do things while we sleep. Like . . .

"Hey, brain. Would you please . . .

. . . find a metaphor to convey this point in my speech?

. . . create an artistic convention to express a crowd scene?

. . . zero in on what my biggest customers really want?"

The assignment becomes a natural restarting place. With a clear place to begin, we restart feeling confident and focused. We're sucked into the work at the place we left it, synapses firing. In this state, inspiration visits quickly.

Most Starts Are Restarts

They aren't as sexy as that dash out of the starting gate, but restarts are what our creations are ultimately made of. When we look back at our proudest finishes, we see that they're made of a few grand first starts, plus countless restarts.

You see, *not finishing* is not always a *focus* problem; often, it's a reignition problem.

"Finished" is made, quite simply, from day after day of going back to the work.

Masterpieces are made by stopping deliberately and starting again. Of reactivating passion and imagination. Imagine, rinse, repeat.

I'll admit, restarting doesn't always feel creative. Sometimes moving forward on a project is a frustrating shopping expedition of asking questions, putting out feelers, waiting for emails to be returned, begging for emails to be returned . . . then realizing the email will never be returned, and starting all over again with a new approach.

Don't let these moments make your exciting creation feel administrative or like do-over work. Bring your "A" game—your *AGAIN game*.

Instead of just ticking through your to-do list, treat your restart like an ignition session or create an on-demand ritual. Remember, a ritual brings a conscious shift to a state of contemplation. Well-thought-out questions can direct the process. Use questions that give a new shot at clarity, a chance to recalibrate. Like:

What have I learned?

What should I shift or stop?

What problems need attention or new ideas?

How can I make this more fun or important?

Pay attention to your emotional state. Try to tap into the anticipation of your first magical starting stages. Bring zeal, optimism, and curiosity. Trust the creative process.

START UP

START OUT

START IN

START OVER

Restarts After the Fun Parts

In every creation that meets with success, there's a season of restarting that seems to shout, "The fun part is over!" It's that time when entrepreneurs feel less like creators and more like human resources managers, artists feel like shipping clerks, architects feel like contractors, and authors feel like carnival barkers.

Relax your shoulders, check your privilege, and phone a friend. You can do this.

Finding our audiences, building our companies, promoting our podcasts—these are as chock-full of inspiration as any part of our creation. Embrace it all.

If a book falls in the forest, and no one reads it, is it really a book?

Moving my book from just-in-time grad gift to bestseller is a story of restarts I never saw coming. Yes, I wanted to get my book into lots of hands. And, of course, I wanted to recoup my investment. (I don't mind telling you that I had spent thousands of dollars getting the book designed and printed. Not every book costs a lot up front, but mine had art in it, and I made the decision to spring for quality design and printing. I drink cheap wine and never get my nails done, so this was my splurge. You don't need to spend a lot to print your book.)

I took my little book to market and helped it find its audience. I made a website, did social media, all of it. It sold well in independent bookstores and on Amazon through graduation season, and sales spiked in back-to-school season. Then, sales stayed strong through the fall, when it became popular for college care packages.

I was thrilled. My publishing company and its staff of one did a bang-up job. Within a year, I had recouped most of my investment.

The better my self-published book sold, the more I wondered what would be possible with the muscle of a mainstream publisher behind it. I had heard stories of self-published books being picked up by publishers once they were selling well—*Rich Dad Poor Dad* and *Fifty Shades of Grey*, to name two. It had worked for financial guidance and a steamy novel, so why not for wholesome snarky motherly advice?

I poked around on the internet and inquired with some agents to learn how many books I would need to sell to get on a publisher's radar. Some agents gave me ridiculously high numbers—in the tens of thousands. Somewhere though, I heard the number 7,000, an oddly specific number, and not very scary. I figured there must be something magical about it.

That became my number. I had sold a few thousand already and I just needed to repeat that to get to 7,000. And Christmas was coming! I restarted marketing, reenergized.

Cut to a few months later. I was driving in a snowstorm on highway I-55 South, returning to Kansas City from visiting Tess at DePaul University in Chicago, when my phone rang. It was a Chicago number I didn't recognize. I wouldn't have answered, but I worried it was from one of Tess's friends and that something was wrong. It was a "real" publisher asking if I wanted a "real" publisher.

"Why, yes. I think I might."

Do Your Laundry or You'll Die Alone had sold more than 7,000 copies, but more important, it had been a #1 Amazon Best Seller in its category for a few weeks over Christmas. The publisher who called me had another book in the category that usually enjoyed that #1 slot. It got her attention.

I consulted my lawyer and signed with an agent, a stARTistic friend who was launching her own book agency. We negotiated a contract and the rest is restarting history.

The point of the fable for you aspiring wannabe authors is that my little book *Do Your Laundry or You'll Die Alone* is a happy ending with hundreds of restarts. It contains dozens of pieces of art and 270 writing entries, from one-word entries and paper doll cutouts to mini essays and elaborate paintings, each started on a different day with different inspiration. And none of them thought they would grow up to be a book.

The reason I'm taking so many pages to tell you this story about a little book that you will probably not buy unless you have a daughter graduating from high school or college right exactly now (in which case, it is THE PERFECT GIFT) is that this is a start-packed example of how telling our stories becomes the best part of our stories.

When we act on our ideas, and follow the restarts they lay before us, we arrive at finishes we could never have planned. We also arrive at work. Did

I say "work"? I meant "opportunities to restart our creations to the next level."

Back to YOU and the FUN PART. I lovingly implore you: Start your story. It may be a book or a screenplay or a song or a secret journal. It may be a StoryCorps recording or a TikTok documentary. Start at the beginning. Or start with what you had for breakfast today. Or start with the story about third grade when you couldn't sit still in your seat. Or tell the story of a thing you know or a thing you can do well. Pick a topic that makes you want to begin, and let the process pull you forward.

We're not all writers, but we all have stories to tell.

I've met a lot of people who, in telling their stories, learned they ARE writers. Some even became authors.

Want to try it? How about right now?

I've created a system to turn you into an author in less than an hour. Yes, it's tongue-in-cheek, but get on board. It's fun to say things like, "When I was working on my first book . . ."

Let's do it.

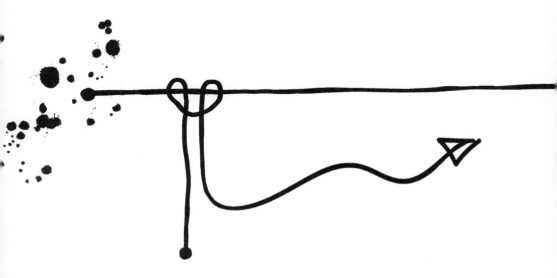

BECOME AN AUTHOR

(20 TO 60 MINUTES)

1. **Decide what kind of book you're writing.** A memoir? A how-to book? A fictional story?

2. **Make your book.** Get a piece of standard printing paper, 8.5 by 11 inches (outside of North America, the standard size is usually 210 x 297 millimeters).

   - Fold it in half lengthwise. Keep the edges lined up straight.

   - Now fold THAT in half.

   - One more time, fold THAT in half.

   - You've folded the paper three times, and it now measures 4.25 by 2.75 inches (11 by 7 centimeters)

   - Hold the long folded edge (the spine of your book) and trim the fold off ALL three other sides, so the pages open freely.

You have sixteen pages—a cover plus twelve pages. You've also learned why, when you print a book, the pages will be a multiple of sixteen. If you add one page, you may as well add sixteen, because you will have to pay for the whole piece of paper. As an author/publisher, you should know this.

3. **Start writing.** Begin on the first right-hand page. (Leave the cover blank for now; you'll write a better title after you finish.) Keep it punchy and to the point. You don't have much room.

To write a "How-To" book, use this format:

Everyone should know how to _____ because _____.

Here's how: (list steps)

To write a mini biography, use this format:

My life has been (*chaotic, action-packed, mundane, unique*).

Take, for example, this vivid memory of (*yesterday's date*).

I woke up at (*time, place*) and then (*write stuff about yesterday*).

How To Become An AUTHOR Before Breakfast
By B. Blades

4.   **Make the cover.** Title your book. I suggest something weird and wonderful that would never make it through the censors. Or, something classic like . . .

How to _____

or

The Story of _____

Write the author name "By (your name)" under the title.

5. **Time to bind!** Staple the spine, or get fancy and sew it using a *single-section binding stitch* you learn on YouTube.

6. **Want to sell your book?** I'd save this collector's item for your kids or a museum, but that's just me. However, if selling out your first book is the bragging rights you're going for, post it on social media with your asking price, and be sure to mention that it's a limited edition.

Congratulations! You're a stARTist, an author, a bookbinder, *and* a publisher! Use your powers for good.

8. IN stARTing ShAPE

Hacks, habits, and creative cross-training to lift more starts

Starting muscles are a secret weapon.

Like the human body, our creative muscle set is an interrelated network of tiny unpronounceable parts that we spend most of our lives ignoring.

Creators each favor different muscles and lean into varying strengths and skills. Visual artists, for example, get comfortable with the creative process: layering, themes, color, nuance, etc. Inventors work in prototypes, iteration, and experimentation. Teachers use language, syllogisms, exposition, and storytelling. Entrepreneurs build skills in assessing risk, marketing, efficiency, product development, logistics, and scaling with success.

Cross-training among these skill sets gives us an edge. Artists and business innovators get this. It's why companies send their product teams to pottery classes, and why artist guilds hold business seminars. Imagine then how cross-training among disciplines can multiply the possibilities for the starting process.

If an idea called for it, we could **imagine** like an architect, **think** through possibilities like a robot designer, **decide** like a chef, and **take action** like a comedy improviser.

Do creative muscles work that way? I asked a stARTistic athlete.

Start Like a Heavyweight

Cam Awesome began boxing at age sixteen to get in shape for a prom date and ended up creating a colorful boxing career, with seven national championships, four Golden Glove Awards, and wins at the 2012 and 2016 Olympic trials for the United States.

At age twenty-three, Cam decided on his awesome name when he made a decision to restart his life. Spending too much time with drugs, alcohol, and bad food, Cam was underemployed and unmoored when a friend bet him he couldn't do a twenty-eight-day cleanse.

"By the end of the four weeks, I felt so good, I wanted to keep going—to improve everything," Cam says. So he changed his name, became vegan, and began training for a boxing career.

After a youth deprived of attention, Cam started learning in his twenties to create the attention he had craved. First, he earned acclaim for winning boxing matches. Then, the confidence he built unearthed a talent for humor. Cam hammed it up in media interviews after boxing wins, playing to the crowd and the camera. Fans loved it.

And Cam loved making people laugh. Before long, he was performing at open mic nights at comedy clubs.

As the word got out that this funny heavyweight boxer was a vegan, Cam was invited to emcee vegan conferences. All the while, his boxing career moved from match to match to championship. Eventually, at age twenty-eight, Cam admitted to himself that he loved the creativity of performing more than the boxing ring, and he decided to take time off from competitive boxing to build a speaking career.

A big part of Cam's motivation to get in shape had come from being picked on as a kid. He knew that his experience was something a lot of kids could relate to. So he wrote a presentation about bullying and self-esteem and pitched it to high schools.

Schools don't have big budgets, so he kept his travel costs and his prices low. He even created a not-for-profit to help schools who could not afford his fees. "If I'm in a city with a paying gig, I also find a school that can't afford me, and present for free. It's the right thing to do, and it helps me build stage time," Cam explains.

For a year, Cam traveled the country, speaking, building relationships, and using skills he learned in boxing to build a speaking business. In his first year, Cam gave presentations to 209 urban schools, a jaw-dropping number for a first-year presenter.

Cam's creative initiative and quick wins made me wonder: How might boxing have impacted his success in speaking?

He says it's all cross-training.

READING THE ROOM. Cam's first audience was fight fans screaming for blood around a boxing ring. Next, it was boozed-up late-night audiences at comedy clubs on open mic night. Then tweenagers. "I learned to respect each audience and to look for techniques that would transfer," Cam says. "I never know when a trick I learned at an outdoor vegan conference can apply to a rowdy comedy audience."

STAGE SKILLS. Time on stage is the best training for time on stage. For Cam, handling hecklers and restless kids, playing to opportunities, and thinking on his feet are all strengths built by being on the stage, responding to what comes at him.

SNAGGING MATERIAL. Cam keeps his imagination in motion, consciously engaging with ideas. "If I'm not performing, I'm looking for material," he says. "I observe. I listen. I put notes on my phone constantly." Cam makes a habit of repurposing ideas—a cooking metaphor becomes a podcast question. A training idea becomes a social media post. After-fight trash talk becomes material for an anti-bullying speech.

FACING DOWN FEAR. When ideas come from a good, creative place, the only reason not to act on them is fear, Cam says. "I got in shape to rid myself of the fear of being physically harmed. Now my only real fear is of being embarrassed." The response to fear and embarrassment are the same, he says: Prepare, then decide not to care.

HOPPING UP AFTER A PUNCH. "After you get dropped with a punch in boxing, you get an eight count . . . eight seconds. If you get up in two seconds, you get eight seconds to pull it together," Cam explains. "If you're down ten seconds, you lose the round." Cam says he applies this decision-making to his creative work. When we get knocked down, hopping up MUST become an instinct, he says.

Cam's cross-training paid off. In March 2020, the coronavirus pandemic abruptly closed schools and comedy clubs. Vegan conferences were canceled. Cam's livelihood evaporated overnight.

He took a knee and eight seconds to gather himself.

Then, he parked in Portland, Oregon, where he started three podcasts, a line of reusable telescoping drinking straws, and a new romance with a school counselor he had met on his last speaking gig.

As the year played out—a year of divisive politics and social conflict—Cam tried to rebuild his speaking business online. Vegan conferences and school assemblies were not ready to go virtual, but Cam bumped into a new opportunity. Businesses needed help bringing employees together and learning about bias and diversity. This was a topic Cam knew something about.

Though he had avoided dwelling on it, Cam, a Black man, had firsthand lifelong experience with implicit bias, and his experience talking to kids had given him techniques for connecting with audiences on the most sensitive subjects. He dug into the topic, wrote a curriculum, and within weeks launched a new speaking series that tripled his income with online presentations.

Cam had no brand in this new field. No connections. He had never presented to a corporation. But he was on his feet and didn't hesitate.

This is what he'd been training for.

When we stretch our skills, we cross-train without even thinking about it. And we up our chances that we'll be in shape for ideas that come at us fast.

What are your stARTistic skills? Which muscles or flexibilities give you an edge? Which strengths do you use in one arena that could improve your game in others?

Creative Cross-Training

All big ideas eventually require tasks that are creations in and of themselves: websites, marketing materials, research, exhibitions, meetings, presentations. All take skills that can be learned with practice.

Why not cross-train with starts that will move your other projects forward?

Do one of these EVERY WEEK:

A CONVENING. Bring people together. Big starts take meetings and collaborations, which can stall creators. We can be shy or unsure about how to engage others. Maybe we don't think we deserve their help. Mostly, we're just out of practice. Practice in small ways. Invite acquaintances to coffee. Throw a happy hour meetup for investors, patrons, or other stARTists.

A QUERY. Create a question and find the answer. Curiosity comes naturally to stARTists, but getting answers is a skill we must build. It takes creativity to pose a good question, and to follow up to get valuable responses.

Ask your customers why they buy the small size of your product instead of the large. Find out whether the demand for pistachio ice cream is on the rise or in decline. Poll your friends to find the best and latest podcasts.

A SYSTEM. Write up and/or illustrate a system, to make it simple and easy to explain to others. Step by step, how do you do it? This is important training. We can start more if we can be efficient and keep track of things—systems and processes help.

A HANDIWORK. Make something with your hands. That's all. Use the skills you have—or even better, try something new. Sketch a sketch. Carve a coaster. Fold an origami swan. Get your hands out and use them. The finger bones are connected to the brain bones, and don't let them forget it.

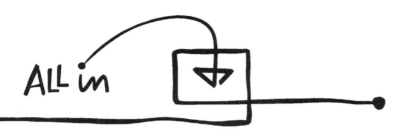

ALL in

All-In Starting

Saying yes to a stARTistic training opportunity is like going to the gym. It's best if you don't think about it too much. You put on your shoes and go. As far as I can remember, this is why I went to Startup Weekend.

Startup Weekend is a fifty-four-hour anybody-can-play event for designing new businesses, held annually in more than 150 countries. My then client, the Ewing Marion Kauffman Foundation, was a sponsor of Global Entrepreneurship Week, which hosted Kansas City's fourth Startup Weekend. So in the name of client research, I signed up.

Seventy people paid $80 each to work over the weekend, from 7 p.m. Friday to 3 p.m. Sunday, teaming up with strangers to build a business from scratch and to have it judged by experts.

It's hard to design robots or make beer in fifty-four hours, so the businesses most teams create are internet-based. In two days, they research, design a business model, conceptualize products, establish a brand, and begin to market it. Some companies are prototyped and coded to go live by Sunday afternoon. Some even make money that weekend.

Kind of puts a sock in your whining about that company retreat, doesn't it?

Startup Weekend begins with a pitch session. In our event, each participant held a posterboard sign of their proposed business name and made a sixty-second pitch. We then voted on ideas using a tried-and-true sticky-note voting system: Everyone got three sticky-note votes.

Ideas with the fewest sticky notes (that would be mine) were encouraged to face reality ASAP and look around for another concept to get behind. At the end of the energetic thirty minutes was born a motley collection of teams, aligned not so much by interest in a particular business idea as by the team leaders' abilities to recruit and refuse people.

I began Startup Weekend with the right motives, but with a wimpy commitment to my own idea. I wanted to create an online clearinghouse for vetted business ideas, a place serial entrepreneurs could list ideas they didn't have time to get to, so others could find those ideas and start them. The idea was fuzzy, and the business model was weak. I wasn't buying it myself, which came through loud and clear in the skimpy showing of sticky notes.

I wiggled my way onto a team with a young stARTist named Royce Haynes and his concept, Dawgbnb, a site to match pets needing boarding with dog lovers willing to take in canine guests for a fee. I thought the idea had legs—at least four furry ones (ha!)—and it sounded fun.

So our team—me and five strangers (three tech guys, one other marketer, and one project manager)—grabbed a table and a pizza and decided on roles, deliverables, and deadlines.

By then it was after 10 p.m. A few team members stood, gathering their things. "Fabulous," I thought. "I'm exhausted." Reaching for my car keys, I saw them settle at a nearby table. They weren't leaving, just moving to get more room.

It wasn't bedtime. It was starting time.

So there it began. All in. Full speed. Think of the most intense caffeine-fueled college group project, and add adults. No one looked at the clock. No one texted their girlfriend. It was a beautiful thing.

I may not have mentioned that the average age of participants was thirty. I was forty-five. They weren't my employees, and I wasn't in charge, as I was used to being. I spent the weekend feeling challenged, and alive.

Saturday started early and ended late. Sunday started early and ended at 3:00 p.m. with team presentations.

Dawgbnb didn't have any customers by presentation time, but the business model and website were amazingly complete. Royce made a tight technical presentation, and pictures of pooches in every frame entertained the judges. Dawgbnb tied for third place. THIRD PLACE out of fourteen innovative business starts!

We accepted our winnings—a package of free legal services—said goodbye to our teammates, and went back to our weekday jobs feeling like start-up whiz kids.

In the days that followed, some team members pushed hard to keep the band together and build out a true launch of Dawgbnb. Alas, after days of texts and emails, it was clear we could not, or WOULD NOT, break from our real lives to give the idea what it needed.

We parted ways, and it wasn't long before someone else launched a practically identical platform idea: Rover.com. That company, A Place for Rover, was valued at $1.63 billion in a 2021 market capitalization. Ouch.

Getting to a big idea first only pays off when you're in shape to give it the restarts it needs.

Some go to Startup Weekend with painstakingly vetted business ideas; some hatch ideas on the drive to the Friday night pitch session; still others come hoping to latch onto a sexy start-up conceived by someone else. A few confess they come merely to tap into the energy and talent pool.

Some, like me, see Startup Weekend as the best kind of stARTistic workout: boot camp immersion. Fast imagining. Fast thinking. Fast deciding. Fast action.

Immersive starting experiences build and stretch us like nothing else. If you're

craving an all-in creative plunge, you'll find a smorgasbord online: storytelling courses, joke-writing workshops, culinary boot camps, interior design workshops, robot design camps, game design courses, ideation escapes, bookmaking weekends, memoir-writing retreats, songwriting workshops, poetry and screenplay workshops, and all manner of fine arts escapes.

Arrive at these experiences ready to create, not just talk. Good workshops will help you play your hardest and learn by doing, and most of them make sure you take home finished work.

If you can't find the immersive experience you want, I guess you'll need to start your own.

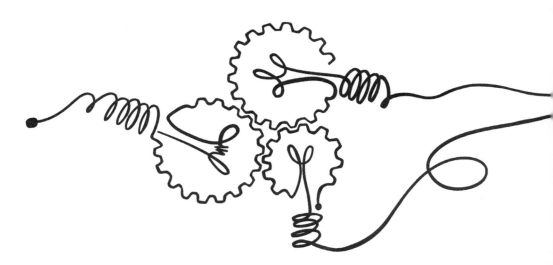

This Calls for a stARTnership

Do you have an idea that needs a lot of something you don't have? Specific knowledge, skill, experience, or access? If this is the only thing keeping you from starting, maybe you need a stARTnership.

Partnerships may last a lifetime, but a stARTnership needs only to get us through the start-up phase.

You can . . .

- **Partner with a pro.** Let's say you're starting something in a field that's new to you, something with a known technology, something where experience will speed things up and keep everybody safe. Unless you have consultants on call, do us all a favor: Partner with an expert, someone who knows the ropes. You bring the "Let's do this!" and let them bring the "Here's how."

- **Partner with a rookie.** On the other hand, sometimes knowing too much can hold us back. Serial entrepreneurs confess that after tasting big success with a business or two, starting something big gets harder, for two reasons: First, we aren't as hungry as we once were. And second, we now have more to lose—money, reputation, relationships, self-respect—you know, ALL the stuff.

  Use the strategy that makes the *Shark Tank* sharks (or titans) swim so fast: Partner with a rookie. A younger, less experienced partner may lack some know-how, but they make up for it with a nothing-to-lose go-getter appetite, commitment, and focus.

  It's not that you CAN'T do it all, but when you don't HAVE TO, why not team up? This works in organizing not-for-profits, building buildings, digital development, you name it.

- **Partner with another skill set.** People with no musical ability write songs. People with scant writing ability author books. And people with no business experience build empires. It happens every day. They find collaborators. Do your homework about the roles and skills you're looking for before you make a commitment.

FORM A STARTNERSHIP

(THIS COULD TAKE SOME TIME, BUT IT MAY CUT YOUR
WORK IN HALF.)

1. **Think of a small something you would not do on your own**, but you'd like to do nonetheless. Can't think of anything? Try one of these:

   - **Create a recipe.** One person brings the cooking skills, one brings the fresh ideas and the sous-chef energy.

   - **Throw a party.** One person brings the theme and atmosphere, one brings the menu, and you collaborate on getting people there.

   - **Make big art.** Some art was never meant to be done alone; collaborate on a lawn sculpture, street art, a marching band.

   - **Launch a co-op.** Food co-ops are fun, but also consider art co-ops, compost co-ops, construction co-ops. Once you get it going, the maintenance team is in place.

   - **Put on a show.** Performer, meet producer. The onstage passion needs backstage energy, and nothing is more fun than a show.

2. **Meet with your potential creative partner** and talk through the idea: What do you both imagine, think, and decide about your project, and why would you make a good team?

3. **Define the terms of your collaboration.**

   - What does success look like?

   - What's in it for each of you?

   - What are you each willing to invest?

   - Set roles and ground rules, such as how/when/why will you meet?

   - Once the idea is launched, how do roles change?

4. **Show up and start.** Take action while excitement is high, and bring your best game. Use the experience to imagine the possibilities for future stARTnerships.

The Art of the Small Start

When an already jam-packed life makes us afraid of adding one more thing, we find ways to swat away even our best ideas. We sideline our sense of possibility and arrive at "Nope, not today."

That's when we turn to the **art of the small start**.

I derive this from the "small step" or Japanese Kaizen method, a popular tool in business processes, athletics, psychotherapy, and medicine, and in changing all manner of personal habits.

Here's the trick. Instead of starting with a grand, explosive, decisive starting session, we begin in the smallest way possible—with the teeny tiniest step we can imagine. An act so small, it's nearly impossible to put off. Then, we restart daily with small next steps. The art is in finding that bite-size morsel to begin with. Let's try.

- A writing project? Write one sentence.
- An art project? Sketch for one minute.
- Writing a song? Write three measures.
- Starting a business? Source one competitive product or service and pop it on a Pinterest board.
- Starting a book club? Text one potential member to gauge their interest.

If you can't yet think of a way to chunk up your project, **start by listing tiny morsels of times and locations** you could use to create, without stress: five minutes in bed in the morning, three minutes waiting for a meeting to start, or that fifteen minutes when you sneak to the bathroom to get out of doing after-dinner dishes.

Use these moments to take small general actions, like writing a few sentences of an idea statement, or defining specific action items, or writing an elevator speech about your idea.

No, the whole creation will not get done this way. But tiny starts slowly shift something in us. If the

project is viable, it will gain footing and reduce our anxiety about it fitting into our lives. We'll stay connected with the idea and whatever inspired it. Just like with bolder starts, the first step will show us the way forward.

Habit Forming

The people in the best condition usually have habits to explain it, usually habits they built deliberately themselves. Maybe that should be your next creative start.

Habits are all custom-made of 1) triggers, 2) routines, and 3) rewards. Some we choose, some we don't. Most of us have bad habits as evidence. Conversations with stARTists suggest that the habit of creative initiative is built by

1. Starting lots of things

2. Finishing lots of things

3. Building rewards into starting and restarting

Now that you know how to create on demand, to start and restart, you have the ingredients to build stARTistic habits. Grab your ritual and follow these steps.

1. **START THINGS.** Start little things. Start big things. Start important things and trivial things. Train your mind to act on your best creative impulses. If your mind says, "I should write a note to that barista who made my day," then write the note. And while you have the notecards out, write a thank-you note to your mom for teaching you to write a thank-you note. She'll like that. Let your mind equate having an idea with starting an idea.

2. **FINISH THINGS.** No, I haven't forgotten the title of this book. We are talking about habits now, about the things we do without thinking. Your brain needs to expect to finish, to correlate starting with creating and completing. It's the perfect biofeedback loop.

    Train by leaving the starting gate and crossing the finish line in one sitting. Look for small things you can finish fast. Poets, write rough limericks or haiku. Artists, do mini sketches and tiny abstracts. Chefs, make some dip recipes. Knitters, who doesn't love a cup cozy?

3. **BUILD IN ANTICIPATION.** Treat starting like dessert. Create an experience you'll look forward to. Then savor it. Schedule starts as social activities or as solitary retreats. Start things on vacation. Hold starting sessions with upbeat people. You do you.

When we build good habits and the ability to start on a dime, amazing things happen. We lose the anxiety that we used to get from having too many balls in the air, or from leaving things unfinished. We initiate more, and we trust ourselves to know how to restart or stop as our creation demands. Before we know it, the word gets around the universe and ideas are coming at us like five-year-olds chasing an ice-cream truck.

When this embarrassment of riches comes your way, I want you to be ready. Here are some hacks, processes, and philosophies to start more, start better, and FINISH MORE BETTER . . . if that's what you're into.

Slow-Motion Multitasking

Sure, it's risky to give yourself a manicure while you're driving, but in many ways, multitasking's bad reputation is situational.

Many stARTists have several or dozens of projects ongoing, including some that take years. Writers have books and articles in

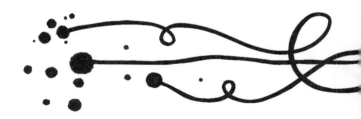

the works while they work full-time jobs as marketing writers; song-writers have arrangements in the works for months or years; my art studio has more than twenty canvases in progress while I finish the line drawings for this book.

Economist and stARTist Tim Harford affirms that for these stARTists, creativity can be boosted by "slow-motion multitasking"—working on many projects at once over long periods of time, even over a lifetime.

In studying the lives of standout creatives like Twyla Tharp and Michael Crichton, and scientists like Charles Darwin and Albert Einstein, Harford discovered that these stARTists kept many projects active, often taking a break from important projects to rest or stimulate their focus with unrelated work. "It's easier to think outside the box when you're clamoring from one box to another," says Harford.

It's an encouraging reminder for stARTists nervous about juggling big things—like starting a social movement while writing a book and creating a killer red sauce recipe. Or running a company while making a microbrew breakthrough and designing the perfect treetop clubhouse for our kids.

Life can go on.

We can advance our ideas without focusing on them solely and directly–

we experiment, explore, sample, and iterate—just by keeping projects alive and living curiously.

On a small scale, multitasking gives us much-needed breaks—chances to give our brains playtime and solve problems when we're stuck. On a grand scale, multitasking lowers the stakes of each project. If we work on only one idea for five years and that project doesn't meet with quick success, it's hard not to feel like a failure. But with several irons in the fire, we keep hope and momentum alive. We reduce the emotional stakes of each effort.

Start in a Series

One of these starts looks a lot like the other ones. It's allowed.

I've started (and finished) more than 1,200 original pieces of art, which have been sold in galleries and online, or given as gifts. If you had offered me a lottery jackpot to make that many unique pieces of anything, I would have told you, "Whoa, I don't want to work THAT hard or live that long."

But it wasn't hard, and here's one reason why: Most of the art fell into series or collections.

When you do a series, each piece is a fresh creation, but starting decisions are at a minimum. For example, I made a series of whimsical houses, about thirty of them, one right after the other, with bright mixed-media scenes composed of paint, vintage ephemera, paper scraps, and lace. Each was unique and told a different story, but each had the same size canvas, the same horizon line, and ingredients pulled from the same place in my studio.

I started each piece with a similar image: a big house placed on the horizon line. This reduced time and indecision, and anchored pieces with a kindred look and theme. With the base built quickly, I could dive into the unique story of each piece. Working in a series made for a deeper creative experience.

For artists selling their work, a series creates a unified, cohesive body of work that pulls in audiences and shows well. **A series looks professional and authoritative and helps artists build their brands.**

This idea—working in a series—works for more than art. It works for social media content, product design, short stories, and all sorts of fine arts. It works if you're creating second-grade lesson plans or executive speeches. And it works in business, academia, and organizations—rolling out new locations, making system upgrades, even creating policy.

Start in Multiples

Why start one masterpiece when you can start three at the very same time? This could be a series, but it doesn't have to be. It could be pieces that are wildly different—things that don't go together at all.

When I'm working on a mixed-media art piece, especially if it's a commission—that is, something specific ordered by a client—I make a point to start a second piece at the same time. I set it up nearby, out of the way, and not so close that it distracts me. Then, when I have an idea or color I want to try out, or an idea that's too edgy for the person who ordered the commission, it goes on the extra canvas. Both pieces have the overall composition I'm going for, so canvas #2 is not just a scrappy free-for-all. But it's definitely not getting the attention of canvas #1. If canvas #2 turns out looking like corned beef hash, I can live with it. It's a bonus painting.

That's why this tip is for in-shape stARTists. Until you can divide your focus and foist some of your work into creative purgatory, this may be unsettling. But once you get in the groove, it can sharpen your focus and take the edge off the stress of your primary project.

Making in multiples gets more things started, and helps the primary project get finished by keeping momentum strong. Once you get a multiple starting technique down, it's not a big jump to add canvas #3 . . . and #4 . . . Now you're rolling!

Starting in multiples works beyond art. If you're a wood-worker, maybe you make multiples of small projects and donate them to a charity; if you're a seamstress, cut two skirts at the same time, and make gift bags or sachets with your extra fabric while the thread is still in the machine. Writers, when you're working on a big project like a book, decide on some other formats to be canvas #2 and #3—an article, a blog post, promotional material for the book, social media posts, etc. When you come up with lines of prose or ideas that just don't make it into your book, pop them into your notes and deploy them when focus allows. Just park the idea, fleshed out enough that you can go back to it. One of these days, you'll be in no mood to work on your book, which is taking for-flipping-EVER, but finishing an inspired tweet will give the day a creative win.

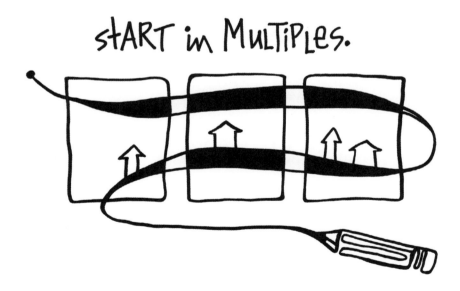

stART in MuLTiPLes.

Start in the Middle

If you're frozen by the intimidation of the first step, or stalled waiting for materials or information, do a workaround. Start in the middle. The middle might be easier, more alluring, or more straightforward. That's what we need—anything to start the action.

Writing a song? Start with the bridge.

Creating a painting? Start from the edges in.

Drafting a speech? Start by writing the last line.

Writing a short story? Start with a central piece of dialogue and work around it.

Planning a business? Start by writing a thank-you letter to your one hundredth customer.

Penning a book? Start by writing the acknowledgments, or a middle chapter, or a random scene where your heroine is running for her life and has to learn how to drive a stick shift in five minutes. This fits in most any story.

Start for the Sport of It

To get good at a sport, we practice specific skills—usually the fun skills that score the points. We do shooting drills in basketball, or go to the batting cage or the driving range. We hit balls one after another. The fun is in the getting better. And the getting better is in the fun.

Creativity training works the same way.

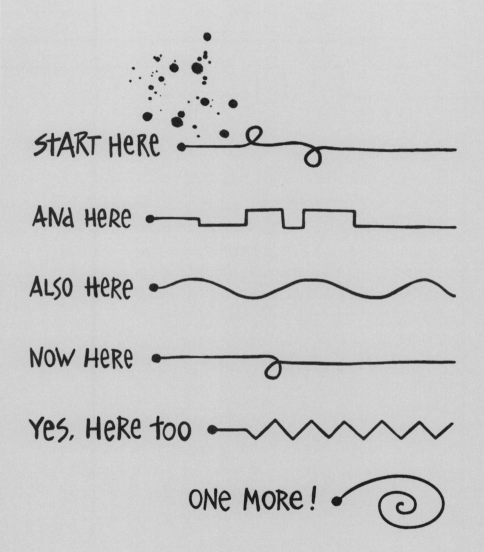

START HERE

AND HERE

ALSO HERE

NOW HERE

YES, HERE too

ONE MORE!

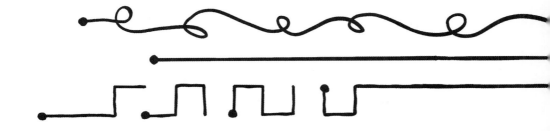

Research shows that creative thinking is boosted by experience, practice, and play.

In his college days, my husband, Cary, wrote country and western songs. When he was most dedicated to his songwriting, Cary practiced a lot. He held his guitar a lot, just strumming and playing with chord progressions. Sometimes he'd put his favorite progressions together with funny, tacky country lines to make singable song titles, like "I Can't Leave Her Behind Alone" or "I'm Under Him Gettin' Over You." Singing these in a medley was his most popular party trick.

As he constructed short, quick pieces, he learned. Sometimes the words came first, and sometimes the music led. He learned how to start pieces within a piece, like a bridge or chorus. He learned that one word was enough to start, and that sitting down with too many ideas was immobilizing. He learned that if one idea took too long, he could go to another one, because no one was keeping score.

Writing titles to music became Cary's version of going to the batting cage. He started songs that he knew would be only starts. Over and over, he played for fun, to practice, and to feel himself getting better.

For filmmakers, the playful practice might be TikTok videos. For business innovators, it might be designing wacky product spin-offs. The crazy thing is, every once in a while, these practice hits wind up flying out of the park.

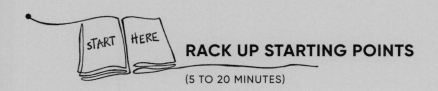

RACK UP STARTING POINTS

(5 TO 20 MINUTES)

1. **Load your stARTistic pitching machine.** List things you can start over and over, and things you'd enjoy starting often. Things like sketches or drawings, lines of dialogue, product ideas, soup recipes, jokes, book or article titles, or tiny abstract paintings.

2. **Get supplies in place**, so you can pop in to practice on a moment's notice.

3. **Log your practice time or number of starts**, if counting is your jam. It's a game, after all.

4. **Schedule your first practice session** or go ahead and take a swing right now.

Creativity thrives with play, practice, and experience.

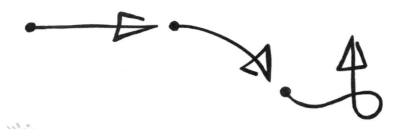

You're Ready

Don't let all this talk about training make you think you're not ready with the starting muscles you already have. If you have an idea, if you put it through its paces, if it lands on you and clings to you, chances are you have everything you need to begin.

Our imaginations know our capabilities, even better than we do. You could not come up with the idea if some part of you did not believe you could bring it to life.

Inherent in the IDEA is the ABILITY to START iT.

9. START SUPPLIES

How to trap inspiration with tape, power tools, and YouTube

Lying beside her at bedtime one night, I asked my then four-and-a-half-year-old daughter, Tess, why she was examining her fingernails so closely.

"I'm deciding whether they're ready to bite off," she said.

"Oh."

"Fingernails are good stuff, you know," Tess said matter-of-factly.

"Oh, really?"

"Yes, you could MAKE something out of them," she said.

"Like what?" I asked.

"I don't know, but I'm saving a collection in my backpack for when I think of it."

I want a parenting medal for not jumping out of the bed immediately and chucking the backpack in the fireplace.

Tess never figured out what to make with her fingernails, but later that week she found her way into my messy studio and emerged with a stunning pair of cloth and string earrings made from my scrap box. She knew I saved good stuff, and she knew where to find it.

Of all the things I've done as a parent, I'm most proud of the fact that I kept scissors in every room and I kept art supplies where the kids could reach them. And I'm proud that my kids, now grown, understand that the best art supplies don't come in cellophane from the art supply store. At our house, art supplies took the form of broken jewelry, scraps of old clothes, used wrapping paper, and Barbie doll legs.

And, it seems, fingernails.

The world is a creative playground. Supplies and muses are all around us.

Creative Collecting

Spotting and keeping things that catch our eye and spark our imaginations—it makes us look at our world with an eager hunger and gives us a treasure seeker's glee for things we might otherwise walk right by. This collector's impulse directs us to save shards of beauty and moments that are uniquely ours.

That's why you rarely see a highly creative person worry about where to get stuff to make stuff. More often, they have the opposite problem. Curious minds can struggle with collecting and hoarding, with dragging things home.

Driving home late one night, artist Lisa Lala spotted a dull glistening on the shoulder of the busy highway. So curious was she, that she circled back after two exits to harvest what turned out to be a yards-long bent-up piece of shiny strapping metal. "I had it on the floor of my studio for months until one day inspiration broke through. I hung it on the wall and started working." The "tangle," as Lisa titled it, birthed months of ideas and successful series of sculptures and paintings.

I drag home smaller trash—offbeat ephemera like old documents, fabric, machine parts, and vintage doll appendages. These tidbits show up in works of art that emerge years later. A wartime love letter from the flea market inspired a mixed-media series, a wing-shaped morsel of driftwood inspired a garden mobile, my childhood paper dolls inspired a painting series. While they wait for duty, my collections hang from clothespins or lie stacked on bookshelves in ways that amuse me.

That's the secret of creative collecting. **If an object gets to you, just hanging or sitting there, it's moving something in you. Eventually, it will get you moving.**

Visual artists aren't the only creative collectors. Writers, speakers, and comedians hoard storytelling scraps. They save ideas and bits of dialogue, like I saved my chat with Tess about her fingernails. I wrote it in my journal the second she drifted off that night.

I've been pretty proud of myself for holding on to ideas, mostly in journals, organized by trips or years. But I was humbled when I read David Sedaris's books *Theft by Finding: Diaries (1977–2002),* and *A Carnival of Snackery (2003–2020),* a magnum opus of journal harvesting.

Sedaris pored through hundreds of journals, spanning from his days as a twenty-year-old hitchhiking through Oregon to his years living in New York, London, and Paris, to create hysterical, poignant memoirs. Among decades of entries, Sedaris found, curated, and knitted together unlikely fibers—funny scraps of dialogue he overheard in restaurants, observations from his trash collecting walks, and lists of random names from the phonebook, like "Adonis Labinski" and "B.J. Beefus." *He saved names from the phonebook!*

Yes, Sedaris is an enviable writer and storyteller, but the magic of these memoirs is in the collecting. For a lifetime, he observed and recorded treasures, and he brought them home.

You can almost see Sedaris jotting down moments as they happened, desperate to capture the farce of his reality: "Today I saw a one-armed dwarf carrying a skateboard. It's been ninety days since I've had a drink." You can imagine him chronicling interpretations of personal moments, like when he first met his partner, Hugh: "I got him to say that he hated me, which usually means the opposite. When I turned around to look at him, I saw that he'd turned around as well. It was romantic."

After I read these collections, I started a new journal and resolved to fill it like Sedaris, with quirky snapshots of my days and witty takes on run-of-the-mill moments. Alas, it sits empty, but for two pages I filled at a truck stop in Idaho. Turns out, my days are not that interesting and I'm not Sedaris funny. I can't pull bestselling books out of journal scraps. But let him try to find baby doll body parts in the 3-euro flea market bin. We all have our collecting superpowers.

When we declare ourselves stARTists, we declare ourselves collectors on the hunt.

We learn to set traps for stuff that inspires us. We buy supplies before we know how we'll use them. We decorate our walls, fill our bulletin boards, and load our electronic devices with reminders of why we love what we love to make.

Some of us learn to catalog our collections and ideas, so we can find them when we want to start or restart. We learn to cull and curate. Alas, we learn to live with a little more mess, and to delight in the process of accumulating, sorting, creating, and discarding.

As we learn to access the materials of our creations, we come to trust that there will always be more when we need it . . . that inspiration and art supplies are like fingernails—wait awhile, and more will grow.

Organizing Treasure

A stARTist's most valued supply stash is their personal collection of inspiration. A screenshot here, a fabric swatch there, a juxtaposition of street grit captured in a photo . . . we harvest what excites us, to tap its power later.

The trick is the "finding it later" part.

Organizing systems can be hard work; some border on creative rituals. And some are more storage than organization—stARTists do what works for them.

- Book designer Ben Denzer archives daily on his website, posting a single composite image of photographs and screenshots taken that day along with one quote he heard or read.

- Chef, inventor, artist, and entrepreneur Laura Laiben files ideas based on the type of creativity she's trying to foster— recipes, art, clothing design, etc. She collects photos and text inspiration in a digital file, and moves items to a small paper journal as they transition to active projects.

- Sculptor Tom Corbin pulls images from art and fashion magazines and pins them to the wall with sketches and notes, and he fills legal pads with designs and production ideas.

- Filmmaker Gigi Harris keeps a customized inspiration play-list on YouTube to capture techniques, music, color, and things that make her laugh.

CAPTURE YOUR INSPIRATION

(30 MINUTES TO 1 YEAR)

1. **Write about how you get inspiration.** Are you visual? Musical? Tactile? How so?

   Do the words of others—quotes, dialogue, prose—activate something in you? Are you inspired by travel or group experiences? Do memoirs and personal profiles appeal more than fiction? Does reading science or history ignite ideas?

2. **Start collecting your inspiration** in the simplest way possible, while you create a system you love. I suggest a large accordion folder, using tabs as you see fit. Or a box.

3. **Do what comes easy, and look for patterns.** Do you like looking at Pinterest in the evening? Do certain artists or bloggers publish things you like? Do you like saving images digitally or on paper?

4. **Research organizing tools and methods** for your work style and interests. Go online to find software tools, reviews, and people on social media who actually use tools. The exploration alone can inspire.

5. **Decide on a system**, based on your research. Transfer the items you've accumulated into your new system and use it for six months. If you're not liking it or using it, go back to the accordion folder or box. Sometimes that's all you need.

This exercise may be the first step of a yearslong process. Enjoy it! And keep it simple.

Supplies, Tools, Muses, and Mentors

I don't believe in waiting for "the creative urge" to strike, but if I did, I'd tell you to prepare for a creative urge like you prepare for the apocalypse:

- Know what you'll need
- Know how to get it
- Know how to use it
- If possible, keep it where you can grab it before the bad guys come

My theory is this: in a busy life, we can all be like seven-year-olds with ADD. (I can make this joke because I was a seven-year-old with ADD.) If we wake up with an idea, and our crayons are in a basket beside the bed, we'll be shoving a drawing in Dad's face before he finishes breakfast. If, however, the crayons are locked in a box in the hall closet, we'll head for the hall closet, trip over yesterday's jeans, knocking a candy wrapper out of the pocket, reminding us that Halloween is next week and . . . crayons are no longer the destination.

Get things in place to start quick, easy, and often. Fill your shelves with the stuff your starts are made of. Even if your creating does not usually involve making stuff by hand, stock some basics.

I happen to think all humans need art supplies in every room for our entire lives. At the very least, we need something to *write with* and *on*, something to *cut with*, and something to *stick things together with* (tape or glue). That way, when we have an idea, we're seconds away—not a trip to the store away—from acting on it. We're seconds away from our freshest take.

Yarn for knitters, wood for woodworkers, fabric for sewers and designers, spices for cooks. Thread, paint, mediums, ink, paper, pigments, polymers, clay, surfaces, nails, rope, and wire nearby can be a reason we start or the reason we don't.

Having materials at the ready is *not even the best thing* about stocking start supplies. Like our creative collections, start supplies become muses and mentors. Just sitting on a shelf, they invite and tempt us. When we pick them up, they nudge and teach us. They show us how to start.

The same goes for tools.

Cam Awesome texted me one day, "What have you done to my girlfriend? She's out buying power tools." Oops. His partner, Kelly, was on an off-road creative adventure called furniture upcycling, and I had maybe somewhat sort of hinted that a variable speed reversible drill would rock her world. It did.

For stARTists, all tools are power tools. The objects that help us craft seem connected to a universal energy source. They bring confidence, leverage, speed, and ideas.

Our stARTistic destinies may well depend on the tools we're exposed to.

If you grew up puttering beside your dad in his workshop or garage, you opened some possibility portals the rest of us may never see. If you learned to work a sewing machine or set of chef knives at a tender age, you have a creative advantage. Use it. (Let's take a moment of silence to mourn high school Shop and Home Ec classes. Sigh.)

If a particular tool intrigues you, there's probably a reason. Maybe your brain is making a connection and a natural aptitude is calling. (Someone gave me a Dremel tool one summer and I didn't come out of the basement for twelve hours.) Find a way to safely learn what a new tool does. Take a class. Watch a tutorial. Talk to the folks at the hardware store, art supply shop, or music store.

A router, a guitar, tiny baking tins, fountain pens, a glue gun, a staple gun, a rolling pin, a press, a wood lathe, a camera, a palate knife, a trowel, a vintage typewriter, a soldering iron, a loom. These are answers stARTists gave me when I asked them to name an object that made them want to make something, just by seeing it.

If it doesn't overwhelm you, keep your tools where you can see them, for maximum access and inspiration. Sure, it's a challenge to make screwdrivers fit your dining room aesthetic, but I've seen it done. If you have the luxury of space, turn over a room or garage to your own stARTistic workshop vibe, hanging tools and materials and using shelves instead of drawers, so you can see and grab everything.

When I suggest you stock your home with start supplies, again, I don't mean only visual tools. I mean musical instruments, computer technology, microscopes, woodworking tools, and whatever you use to create.

The same goes for our workplaces. If I were running things, every company would have an art studio, musical instruments in the break room, and a resident sketch comedy troupe. If you agree, put a note in the suggestion box, and maybe don't push it. These may not be your hills to die on. But definitely do ask for the supplies you need to be creative at your job—like inviting technology, R&D resources, easy-to-use presentation systems, and training, training, training.

Only when you can dabble, experiment, and express your best ideas can you bring the creative initiative that businesses say they want.

People, Places, and Cheering Sections

Sadly, the most important starting resources will not fit in our go bags. Some, you might discover, are spaces:

- Inspiring locations
- Private, quiet retreats
- Makerspaces
- Outside workshops—welding studios, woodshops, recording studios, printmaking studios, etc.

By far, the most valuable, empowering resources are other creative beings. And we need a lot of them.

- Collaborators
- Supportive relationships
- Go-to talent pools to delegate to
- Creative groups and gatherings
- Teachers and mentors
- Interesting friends and acquaintances

To leave the best of ourselves in the world, we must stock our lives with intimate connections and a lifelong stream of new, interesting acquaintances. No other source inspires or stimulates as well as people.

As a practical matter, we need people to help launch our ideas as partners, collaborators, funders, talent, and staff. We may need customers or patrons.

And whether we sell our work or not, we also need fans. We need people to respond to what we make. We need people to listen to it or read it or eat it or wear it or climb it or ride it or swing from it.

Art craves an audience.

Maybe you don't think of your next stARTistic creation as art. But in some way, your creation—the thing you start from scratch and make the way only you can make it—that thing will be a work of art. And art craves love, attention, and understanding. We all want our work to be seen and liked. That's part of it.

For stARTists, ambitious or not, part of the journey is putting our starts out there to sniff around and find the people who like them. Every stARTist's work won't be for everyone, but it won't be for no one. Find your someones.

As my third-grade teacher said while helping me find a new friend when Janet with the go-go boots moved away after Christmas break, the best way to FIND a someone is to BE a someone.

HOST A STARTIST SALON

(1 MONTH+)

1. **Pull together a gathering of stARTists** in your life and community. Keep it diverse. If you're a musician, don't invite only musicians. Include a business owner, a teacher, a poet, a chef, a filmmaker. Use this chance to meet people you've admired or been curious about.

2. **Tap a good host.** Salons stimulate conversation, exchanges, and inspiration. They're best with a strong host who guides the discourse. If you're not comfortable doing that, include a friend who is.

3. **Ask questions to get conversation flowing, like . . .**

   • What are you working on now?

   • Do you have a process for starting new projects?

   • How do you treat a new idea when you're in the middle of something else?

   • How do you feel about your unfinished work?

4. **Steer conversations toward cross-training.** What does a musician do to take a song into a new arrangement? How does a ceramicist come back from glaze mishaps and kiln explosions? How does a business owner pivot when a product goes out of fashion? How does a poet restart every day? How does a community organizer regroup after the election is over?

10. The STAKES of OUR stARTs

Placing bets on timing, skills, risk, and ideas only we can start

Even as we resolve to become the best stARTists we can be and get things in place to start more and create better, we may notice ourselves holding back.

A few causes are worth mentioning.

To begin with, some of us are flat-out idea hoarders. We're terrified of using our best ideas until *we're* ready and *the idea* is ready and *the world* is ready and we can afford an idea insurance plan. We hold back on starting until we're locked and loaded with every resource on hand. We don't want to use the "big" idea until we have the time to go "all in." Or we don't want to use energy on smaller ideas that might not win the big payoff.

Take my friend Jane, who asked me not to use her real name or her real idea. Jane has a fun side-hustle business idea, and she's afraid she will never have an idea as good as this one. She fears if she starts it now, if she spends the idea before she's ready, it won't pay off, and she'll be broke. Idea broke.

That's not even a thing, Jane.

Ideas don't work like that. Ideas are multiplying, self-perpetuating wonder weeds. By the time you spend one idea, another is already growing. It's annoying, really.

Successful stARTists turn ideas into starts and spend them all. And they never run out. They might even squeeze multiple starts out of a single idea.

Spend your ideas like a drunken sailor. Let them burn a big hole in your pocket. Only by spending an idea will you know what it's worth. Only by starting can you birth the next generation of better ideas that come from it.

By the way, one clue that you're an idea hoarder is a stack of pristine unused journals on your bookshelf. What are you waiting for? Do you expect a phone notification when an insight is worthy of writing in your $25 treasure? It's not happening. Grab that journal and write about why you're hoarding journals.

Let's agree not to die with empty journals or unexplored ideas. That's boring. Let's die with journals full of crazy starting stories that turned into crazier starting stories. Those are the people's funerals we want to go to.

Now, if you don't consider yourself an idea hoarder, if you're ready to spend your ideas and pour your starts into the waiting-with-bated-breath world, but things aren't happening in the easy tra-la-la way you imagined, it might be that you need to look deeper. (I know, I hate those words, too.) You might have a demon to wrestle.

Creative demons have been holding back stARTists since the beginning of time. They include

but are not limited to: fear, ego, fraud complex, burnout, denial, bad habits, scarcity attitudes, shame, grief, loss avoidance, anger, resentment, and fear. (Fear is listed twice because . . . you know.)

We've hinted at all of these scoundrels in stories and exercises, but it helps to name them. It puts them on notice.

Read the biographies of your favorite creators and you'll see that every stARTist grapples with some of these. It's a part of the deal. I've often wondered whether that's what our ideas show up to do—out our creative demons, and make us take them on.

If you're truly struggling, please, be quick to get help. Professionals, like therapists, are best if you're in a lot of pain. Creative demons do indeed inflict pain. But you can banish most of them over time by spending time with other stARTists, your journal, and the teachings of experts. And sometimes, just by starting.

Do the work you must to heal your creative wounds and nurture your creative spirit, so you can soak in the fulfillment of the stARTistic life you're meant to live. The sooner the better.

Tick Tock

Creating should be a relaxed, regret-proof, schedule-free state of mind, but initiative has an annoying theme song playing in the background that sounds like . . . tick tock. Creative initiative can be a vexing calling.

I have always believed that **when we act on an idea, we time-stamp it.** Our idea gets that moment in history, and whatever we have to offer it, only then. So when we think about the stakes of acting on our ideas, and of building our lives into the starting machines our imaginations deserve, we have to think about losses and limitations.

What are we losing when an idea goes unexplored? What are we losing when we defer deciding? Or we delay the first step? How much time do we have in this particular piece of skin before our lens changes?

When I rifled through my unfinished work, some days felt rueful. I thought the work I held symbolized missed opportunity, squandered youth. Even after I made peace with my past creations, a few "what ifs" nudged in. Seeing the success of other stARTists showed me what I might have been missing. Though I have no true regrets, if I had a moment with my younger self—that college girl and that twenty-something—I'd push some advice.

I would NOT tell her to finish more. But I might tell her to start more, start differently, and pay closer attention. I might tell her to live in more cities, buy bigger canvases, and use more orange. I would definitely tell her to place more bets.

Stakes are high. Time is short.

Late Starts

One Tuesday a few years ago I happened into an art gallery in a suburban strip mall. Galleries always give me a jolt of ambition, and this one was a favorite, because by day, artists actually painted in the gallery, and by night, it hosted art classes.

At the back of the studio, a tall fifty-something man in a University of Kansas ball cap stood painting at a huge easel. The image taking shape on the massive canvas was consistent with the works on the walls around him: striking colorful figures of vibrant young women, each more beautiful than the next.

The man stepped quickly away from his work to greet me warmly. Breaking concentration can be costly to an artist. But clearly, Bill Rose loved talking with people, and he spoke of his artwork with the guilty delight of someone talking of a fresh love affair. After probing just a little, I got him to tell me a story that, I gotta say, gave me goose bumps.

A successful technology project manager at a big company, he was the father of three athletic girls, and he volunteered as a basketball and softball coach for his daughters' teams. Along the way, he had become a capable photographer, recording family and sports moments and learning to find light and emotion through the lens of a camera.

"One weekend," Bill said, "I was looking through some photos I had taken at a KU women's softball game. My thirteen-year-old daughter was taking an art class at the time, and her supplies were sitting on the table in front of me. I was bored, with nothing to do, so I reached over and grabbed her sketchpad and pencil and began sketching from one of the photos I had taken."

Bill drew what he saw, and within an hour he had a sketch that looked pretty much like the photograph. He showed it to his daughters (ages ten, thirteen, and sixteen) and wife, and they were blown away.

"I was pleased with the drawing," Bill said, "but mostly, I was excited about the fact that drawing was so easy. I remember thinking, 'People don't know how easy this is, or *everyone* would be doing it.'"

Bill eagerly shared his discovery. "I pushed the sketch pad at my wife and said, 'Here, try this, I bet you can do it. Just LOOK at the picture and DRAW what you see.'"

His wife eventually convinced him that no, it was not so easy, and NOT EVERYONE could do it. Clearly, Bill had a real, pure talent.

Bill spent the next months and years in frenzied bliss, buying drawing supplies, selecting subjects to draw, and reading everything he could get his hands on about drawing people, particularly female athletes, the subject of his photography for so many years.

His life since then looks like someone held their finger on the FAST-FORWARD PLAY button of a too-good-to-be-true life story. Juried art shows, awards, fast-climbing sales, doubling prices, enthralled repeat patrons, and prestigious gallery showings fill his days—these are trappings of success that career artists work a lifetime and never achieve.

On that day I met him, more success was unfolding. Bill had just learned that his drawing of his assistant had won a worldwide drawing contest to be selected as the now-iconic cover of the Strathmore Drawing Pad. And he was packing for a trip to Carmel, California, to begin a dream assignment producing the artwork for *The Forger*, a movie with the Clint Eastwood family about an art prodigy who gets pulled into the world of international art forgery.

This man who discovered his talent at age forty-seven was creating art for a film about an artist who discovered his talent as a child.

I ran into Bill a few years later, again working in public on a large canvas. This time, he was working on a mural-size painting celebrating the Kansas City Royals' 2015 World Series Championship. Commissioned by the team itself, the painting hangs in The K, Kansas City's baseball stadium. It seems Bill's background as a coach and sports photographer gives him a sixth sense about creating powerful sports art, and he gets frequent requests to do massive milestone work for stadiums and national sports teams.

Bill doesn't spend time lamenting not discovering his talent for forty-some years. "It may not be a bad thing," he said. "If I had been caught up in my career when I discovered art, I might have thrown it off. Maybe I would not have appreciated it. My art career started at the right time for me."

But I have my own theory about Bill's timing and success.

I think Bill stepped so easily into his life as an artist because he is a lifelong stARTist. He was a photographer, a

student of light, and a seeker of personality in the frame—an artist with a trained eye. His tech job required him to initiate change and create solutions. I also discovered that Bill is a musician who played in a band and wrote songs in his youth. And he's a writer, with a screenplay optioned.

So when Bill discovered his talent for drawing and painting, he didn't ponder or check himself into an art school. His stARTistic muscles were ready for heavy lifting.

Bill's goal now, in his sixties, is to be more stARTistic. "I still struggle with trying new things. It's my aim to experiment more—to take more chances," he said. "I'm almost embarrassed to say that I finish everything I start. I don't have stacks of unfinished paintings lying around like other artists. And maybe I should."

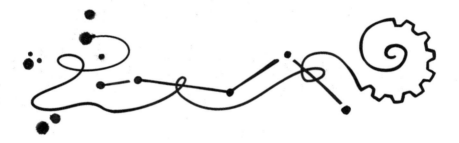

Bill Rose's story makes me wonder what skills might lie in wait for me. It has made me try new things far outside my comfort zone, and wish I had started earlier. Just as I mourn all the ideas that never get started, I now also mourn all the talents that may never be known.

What if you're forty and have never taken piano lessons but always wanted to try? Maybe it will take ten years before you can lead the Christmas sing-along. Or maybe you're a prodigy, two years from a concert stage.

IF YOU'RE
FINISHING
EVERYTHING
YOU'RE STARTING,
YOU'RE
NOT STARTing
ENOUGH.

What if you have a talent you haven't discovered? Have you ever tried sculpting? Or woodworking? Or sewing? What if you're spooky good at composing music or baking soufflés or moving crowds of people to make social change? What if you have a knack for fiction writing? Or blowing glass? Or building squirrel traps? What if your hands are quicker learners than you think they are?

Master of None

Why are we so afraid to look for new skills as we get older or busier? My twenty-two-year-old art students sound just like senior citizens I interviewed. The excuses menu starts like this:

"It would not pay off fast enough."

"I don't have talent in that."

"I don't have time to get good enough."

"I don't have enough money to finish."

"My partner will leave me if I take up more space in the house."

"Who do I think I am?"

I've heard people blame Malcolm Gladwell. (Not me. I think he's a genius.) In his book *Outliers*, Gladwell concludes that mastering a skill takes 10,000 hours of practice. Some people hear that and decide, "I'll never be able to master the ukulele at fifty years old, with a full-time job."

We don't have to be *masters*, though, to enjoy a creative skill. We don't have to be extraordinary or at all accomplished to enjoy an ability.

It always bugs me when someone tries an insult using the quote "A jack of all trades is a master of none." Because they're leaving off the second part of the quote, which goes: "but oftentimes better than a master of one." To me, that's the real point.

A case for stARTistry is a case for generalists. It's a case for learning *something* about a *lot* of things—to allow us to bring more ideas to life.

David Epstein, author of *Range: Why Generalists Triumph in a Specialized World*, says "Our greatest strength is the exact opposite of narrow specialization. It is the ability to integrate broadly."

I'm certainly not a specialist or a master of anything. I've been writing and making art since my teens, and I do well enough to sell my work. Also, I can do light carpentry, weld, sew, garden, and play drums with skill levels from AVERAGE to VERY POOR.

Most of these skills, if you're kind enough to call them that, I learned before I was ten, or after I was forty. All of them I learned because I wanted to make something specific. **I didn't want to get great, I just wanted to get something done.**

Most stARTists I know have a fun portfolio of skill sets, and they're game to hop on a YouTube video to learn something new. One entrepreneur says, "I learned to garden well enough to avoid paying someone else to do it. The same for carpentry. Now I'm building a trellis in my award-winning garden, and it's the most satisfying project I've ever tackled."

Starting new interests is a lifelong feast.

WHeN ~~WHAT~~ ARe YOU WaiTiNg FOR?

Ideas Have Time

What would you start if you knew someone else would finish it?

Throughout history, men have taken bricklaying jobs they knew would last a lifetime, because the building—the cathedral, wall, or mountain carving—would not be done in their lifetime. And the stARTist who began the masterpiece, the person with the vision, inspiration, and courage, knew they would not lay the last stone or cut the ribbon or eat cucumber sandwiches at the grand opening party.

They started anyway.

This is stARTistry for grown-ups. As we worry about running out of time to finish our screenplays while we're young enough to play the lead role ourselves, let's remember that some of the most focused, disciplined creators don't invest themselves in the moment of completion; instead, they invest themselves in the ignition. They invest themselves in fleshing out the idea and getting it rolling.

Ideas aren't mortal. They have more time than we do. If we ignite an idea we don't have time to finish, perhaps we can outsource it. Perhaps we can find someone to share our vision and take it where it's meant to go.

If we can imagine ideas so grand we cannot possibly finish them ourselves, maybe it means we're on to something great.

Tick tock.

You Haven't Missed Anything

It's okay, you haven't missed anything.

If you're coming to an idea you've neglected for a while or coming into your creative own at a late age, have no fear, and certainly no regret. Your timing is perfect.

You didn't miss your moment.

You have arrived at this time with everything it took to get here. This is your moment. If you're too tired for it to be your moment, show up at the same time tomorrow.

You didn't miss your idea's big shot. Your idea has lots of shots. What it doesn't have

is another YOU. As the originator of the idea, it's up to you to find the iteration of your idea that fits in today.

You didn't miss all the great ideas. Ideas will come looking for you.

More than you can start. Get in shape, and keep your eyes peeled.

MAKE A LATE START

(5 TO 20 MINUTES)

1. Complete as many of these sentences as you like.

    If it wouldn't take so long, I would learn to . . .

    If I thought I had talent for it, I would try . . .

    If I could afford to, I would make . . .

    If I had the confidence to, I would . . .

    If I had the right kind of help, I would start . . .

    Do you have ideas that got away? Things you would have made when you were younger or at a different place in life? Write them all down.

2. **Now, pick one that still excites you.** Recalibrate it for your life today.

    What is a *version of the idea* you could start today? Get stARTistic. If it's a novel, maybe it becomes a short story. If it's a social movement, maybe you start with a discussion group. If you once wanted to start a company, but you're near retirement age, maybe you find an entrepreneur to mentor or invest in.

3. **Write ideas for a first step.** How can you bring this idea into being, even in a small way? Come back to this page to explore your ideas and feelings around them. You may discover new ideas, or that you've scratched that itch in another way.

Daredevils Among Us

I sold my public relations business to a stARTist named Pasquale Trozzolo, the son of an Italian immigrant who started a candy store in Chicago in the 1930s. (And the nephew of the guy who put Teflon on frying pans; see page 138.) Pasquale loved his family's business as a child, and starting a business was always something he was going to do. Lucky for me, Pasquale's version of a candy store turned out to be a marketing company, the perfect home for my firm, when I was ready to sell it.

Merging or selling a small company is much like courting for a second marriage. Turning over a business can feel like giving up a baby for adoption. *Buying* a company, I'm told, can feel like adopting a school bus full of other people's kids.

The process can include lots of dates and paranoid character assessment. When selling, you look for a solid citizen who will treat your people well and grow the business, or at least maintain it long enough to pay you.

Pasquale scored high on the solid citizen test. Only one thing raised a flag. He liked to drive race cars—in actual Formula 2000 races; those are the loud, sexy, one-seat cars, low to the ground with the big tires. I was impressed with Pasquale's macho pastime, but deep down, it made me nervous.

How does a guy with an expensive daredevil hobby run a business? Does he go fast and loud and close to the wall? How does a guy like that play it safe with the bottom line? OUR bottom line? To take the risk of selling him my company, I had to get comfortable with how he did risk.

As we pored over balance sheets and business history, I learned that Pasquale risks big, but smart. At age thirty-six, he quit his insurance job, cashed in his 401k, and started a company . . . with young kids at home.

"In the early days of my business, I took as much risk as I could. That's how I knew I was growing as fast as possible," Pasquale says. "I'd get mad at myself if I had any money left in the bank at the end of the month. That meant I wasn't putting enough on the line."

Buying my company was Pasquale upping his ante. He figured he could grow faster by acquiring another company than by organic growth alone.

By the time he walked me through his ambitious growth plan, I was kicking myself for taking so little risk for so many years. And I was ready to give him my chips. I said "yes." All in. We merged companies and antique typewriter collections, and Pasquale's risk paid off. He created a rock-solid multimillion-dollar business that was immediately bigger than the sum of its parts.

Live-on-the-edge stARTists like Pasquale show us an aspect of a risk that plays big in our creations. It's what I call "daredevil risk," and it's exactly what it sounds like.

For daredevil stARTists, risk is not a deterrent or something we tolerate. Often it's part of the appeal. Taking big risks—financial, physical, and reputational—is the inspiration.

stARTists don't just build a tolerance for risk, they build an appetite for it.

An appetite for risk helps us imagine big and unbridled. The more we risk, the more innovative, expressive, and monumental our creations can be. An appetite for risk opens us to ideas that don't show up when we're driving laps in our Smartcar. It forces us from our comfort zone.

It's true in all creative efforts.

Artist Ada Koch says, "Why would I start something I'm already sure will work? What's the fun in that?" After decades of safely painting on canvas, her new risk appetite has ushered in a midlife creative career explosion.

Moved by the rise in urban violence, Ada found herself taking bold chances to raise money and awareness alongside anti-violence activists. One risky idea led to another, and soon she was creating sculptures, events, exhibitions, fashion accessories, and public art installations. "If an idea or collaborator grabs me, I say 'yes' and figure it out later," she says. Some things don't get figured out. That's the risk. Ada estimates a third of her work goes unfinished, a percentage she can live with, because she knows creative payoffs come on their own timetable.

Putting time and materials on the line is child's play compared to the biggest risk—the risk stARTists struggle with most, and the biggest fear they cop to: embarrassment . . . vulnerability . . . loss of reputation or respect.

In twenty-plus years as a public relations professional, I filled a file drawer with stories of big business reputation risks. My job was to assess risks before executives took them, help capitalize on them when they paid off, and minimize loss when things went bad.

So . . . cross my heart, one spring morning I was digging through a boxed-up file of PR crises to find a big impressive executive blunder story to make my point to you about risk and embarrassment . . . when I got a text from my neighbor.

"Can you go for a walk? I want to ask your help with something," she said.

We met up that afternoon.

You'd love my neighbor Diana Kander. She's a lawyer turned consultant and speaker, helping companies innovate and build curious cultures. She's made businesses, books, a political campaign, T-shirt designs, and an app to help married women flirt with their husbands. So yes, a big ol' stARTist.

We walked and we talked, and we walked some more. Diana was stalling. I had not seen this side of her.

Eventually, she told me the favor.

"I'm starting a podcast," she said. "It's designed to mentor women using interviews with female experts. My guest for the pilot is Jackie Huba, author of *Fiercely You*; we'll talk about dancing like a drag queen as a workout, how it can help us feel fierce and unstoppable," she said. "I need you to record me dancing . . . like a drag queen . . . out here."

I hope you know people who don't think dancing in public is embarrassing, but believe me, for Diana, it is. And like a drag queen? It was an act of extreme vulnerability. Add the fact that the video could play to untold thousands on the internet, and this was her worst nightmare.

But I knew what was happening. Diana's a risk-savvy stARTist; she knew she'd get over the embarrassment. She'd done it before. But not answering the call of an idea? That would be hard to live with.

WHAT IF
YOU ARE
YOUR
IDEA'S
ONLY
HOPE?

YOU'LL HAVE STARTS
without FINISHES
BUT
YOU'LL NEVER
Have FINISHES
Without
STARTS.

After walking for thirty more minutes, she pushed PLAY on iTunes. There was music. There was dancing. There was staring. There was stopping to check out the video, and restarting. In twenty minutes, we had footage of two women dancing fearlessly down sidewalks. (What kind of beast would I be to let her do it by herself? Shared embarrassment is half as risky.)

Listening later to the podcast, I learned why Diana chose Jackie Huba as her first guest. "I got physically sick from nerves before giving speeches," Diana said. "If the point of the show is to help women overcome weaknesses, I should start with mine." Epilogue: Diana rarely gets ill before speeches anymore.

As we grow in our creativity, the risk might be the point. Starting things that scare us is the way to rid our creative psyches of things that scare us. As Huba says in *Fiercely You*, the way to banish the fear of other people's judgment is to "strike a pose, embody your power, and tell your critics to sashay away." Like a drag queen.

Most creative risk is not real, calculated risk. It's just a sense of risk, a feeling—one that diminishes with every start we start.

Which brings us back to Pasquale. He's retired now, and do you want to guess his new hobby? Who guessed poetry?

He's quite a poet, actually. He has published collections and books, and he collaborates with artists to create poetry wall art. I call it daredevil poetry. Because given Pasquale's personal brand as soft-spoken, private, and oh-so-dignified (he still wears suits and French cuffs), his poetry puts it all out there. It's intimate and sensuous, sometimes controversial and political. But always true, revealing, and risky.

Of You, by You

I'm not going to tell him, because writers hate it when you tell them what to write about, but I hope someday Pasquale writes a poem about how racing cars and growing up in a candy store makes you a better poet. Now that's a poem only *he* can write.

The truth is, every poem he writes is one *only he* can write. And the business he started is one that *only he* could start.

The same goes for you and me.

What's at stake here, dear reader, is existential. **If you do not act on your ideas, they will not exist.** Not really. Not the way you would have made them.

We have creations waiting within us that **only we** can bring forth—combinations of perspective, skills, timing, and history that no one else can tap.

Only Cam Awesome can create an inspiring presentation for kids about growing up bullied, learning to laugh, and becoming a vegan heavyweight Olympic boxer.

Only Laura Schmidt could put "I am awesome" on socks and build it into the feel-good business her affirmations predicted.

Only my stARTistic blonde friend Cara, and her blonde friend Candi, who both love beer and know how to make videos, could have started the YouTube beer review channel Two Blondes Drink Beer.

Only I could write a book that starts with me cutting autumn leaves for a third-grade bulletin board and ends with me dancing like a drag queen. My mom is so proud.

As you go forth with your story, to start more and leave more of yourself in the world, I hope you won't look so much at what seems to be working for others. I hope you'll start with the things that work for you because they're made of you.

What's your history? What did your parents do with their lives? Did you have pets? Where did you live, and how did it shape you? What were your superpowers and challenges as a teen? As a young adult? Which teachers made you believe in yourself? Did your sister make you perform in a backyard musical when you were three?

What skills do you have to create with? Writing, building, coding, dancing, speaking, planting, composing, cooking, sculpting, drawing, singing, leading, community building, inventing?

What do you feel, believe, and love, perhaps unusually strongly? Do you love snow? Do you detest mosh pits? Do you believe in aliens, but only from outer galaxies? Do you believe in composting? Or that the Beatles were best with Pete Best?

The pieces of you are the ingredients of your ideas.

The pieces of you, those you cherish and those you renounce, got you this far. Together, they form a one-of-a-kind starting place.

START.
the THING
THAT
ONLY YOU
CAN
START.